Thomas
—— the ——
Doubter

I THINK, THEREFORE, I DOUBT!

Thomas Frank Christian

PAGE PUBLISHING, INC.
New York, NY

First originally published by Page Publishing, Inc. 2018

The picture of "The Thinker" is well known as a sculpture done by Auguste Rodin (1840-1917).

ISBN 978-1-64298-893-2 (Paperback)
ISBN 978-1-64298-992-2 (Hardcover)
ISBN 978-1-64298-894-9 (Digital)

Printed in the United States of America

To all people who think and question or doubt
about religion and the meaning of life.
It means they are looking for answers and
not just going along with the flow.

Contents

Chapter 1

Introduction

Hello. This is the story of my life so far. I call it *Thomas the Doubter: I Think, Therefore, I Doubt* because I have always questioned what is going on around me. I was named after Thomas the apostle, who, you remember, wanted to put his finger in the wounds of Christ who had just been raised from the dead. But you may not recall that Thomas was one of the most loyal of the twelve apostles. He was ready to return to Jerusalem when he knew Jesus's life was in danger. He was interested in Jesus's prediction of his death and wanted to know how he and the others could follow him. Once he believed fully, he was on the team and traveled as far as India to spread the word. Tradition says he died there as a martyr about AD 68.

I could have been named after Thomas Aquinas (1225–1274), who wrote his famous *Summa Theologica* ("The Highest Theology") where he claimed to raise ten thousand questions about religion but never a doubt. But as I stated, I do and did have some of the same ten thousand questions but also some doubts, so to be named after him would not have been appropriate in my case. In grade school, the good Saint Joseph nuns asked me who was my patron saint. Once they had me in class, they definitely knew I was the doubter. Now, being a doubter is not really a bad thing. It does not necessarily mean one is losing his or her faith. In fact, doubt is part of faith. Indifference is the opposite of faith. It means the person has no interest in believing. Doubt may not be convenient, but it is seeking the best proof possible and helps to keep people honest. And like Thomas the apostle, once I am convinced, I am with you all the way.

9

Mother Teresa, who is now a saint in the Roman Catholic Church, had doubts throughout her whole life. In her writings she stated that "so many unanswered questions live with me."

As you read this, you must always keep in mind that I thank God each day for my life and for experiencing my opportunity to love.

The subtitle is "I Think, Therefore, I Doubt!" This is taken from my college degree in philosophy when we studied René Descartes (1596–1650). He expressed the famous Latin axiom "Ego cogito, ergo sum"—"I think, therefore, I am." I exist as a thinking being, not as a robot accepting everything other people tell me. I respect all who have taught me over the years, but I like to think things over myself too. It works for me.

What makes me think my life is any different from most people, and why should I bother to write about it? That is a good question. For openers, I went into the Catholic minor seminary at the age of thirteen. I was kicked out at the age of seventeen for being a wise guy and asking too many questions. As you will find out, I had to go back into another seminary for college, then went to the major seminary and was sexually attacked by a roommate. I reported him, and he was expelled. There is more to that story which I will go into detail later. Despite all this, I was ordained a Roman Catholic priest February 2, 1963. After enjoying six years of service to outstanding people, I resigned the ministry. I worked as a priest in Roseville, Hopkins, Glen Lake, and Minnetonka, Minnesota. I resigned because of obligatory celibacy. After living a celibate life for six years, I saw ministers, rabbis, and Eastern Rite and Orthodox priests who were married, doing as much good or more than I did. In time, I received my papers from Rome, releasing me from any priestly obligations. When I was to resign, I announced my decision to my parish at my final Masses. The pastor gave me a reception, and a week later, I was a probation officer for Hennepin County Court Services.

As Garrison Keillor would say, today I am happily married to a strong woman and the father of three above-average children—Craig, Andrew, and Jennifer—and the grandfather of five grandchildren: Anderson Thomas, Abigail Rose, Beckett Jon, Elliott Frank, and Audrey Amelia. Actually, my family is much more than that. My wife is an outstanding, kind, and loving person, and my children and grandchildren are more than I could have ever had hoped for.

I have written three other books, so I am not really a rookie at this business, but far from a pro. My first book is titled *Conflict Management and Conflict Resolution in Corrections*. It was published in 1999 by the American Corrections Association, and I am happy to say that it is on their best-selling list. They have asked me to bring it up to date, and the revised edition was published in 2013. My third book is called *Justice Restored*. It was published in 2005 by Ink Water Press. It is used in a number of criminal justice classes around the country as a case study in the concept of restorative justice. I receive royalty checks from all three books; thus, I have the courage to attempt this autobiography.

Along the way in my life, I have had some great experiences and a few not-so-good encounters. It has been a very interesting life, and I want to share it with you before I go to the happy hunting grounds and the great mystery in the sky. If you are interested, read on. If you are not, have a nice day, and I hope you are having a good life too. Remember, the type of life you have depends on you. I found that out early on. It is not based on God's will. God gives us life, and the rest is up to us.

The Early Years

On October 9, 1937, Ruth Leone Carney Christian and Edward Howard Christian were preparing to host a poker game at their farmhouse at 6400 Twelfth Avenue South in Richfield, Minnesota, a suburb near the city line of Minneapolis. Ruth had had one child who was miscarried, and one was still born. She had given birth to a son, Kenneth Edward, born May 13, 1935. This would be hope-fully her second live birth. Company was coming in the door for the card game when Ruth informed Ed that the birth was too close. Given their past history, they took off immediately for Saint Mary's Hospital in downtown Minneapolis. At 8:33 p.m., a bouncing baby boy was born at eight pounds, thirteen ounces, and I was named Thomas Frank Christian.

Thomas Frank Christian was born on October 9, 1937. His family was preparing to host a poker party when he decided to be born. His father said they gave birth to a joker.

Edward Howard Christian, Tom's father, was a police officer for twenty-seven years and ran a 160-acre farm. He died of a cerebral hemorrhage two months from retirement at the age of 61 and 10 months.

Tom's mother Ruth Leone Carney with Tom's father Edward Howard and four of their children (Ken, Tom, Ed, and Dave) at the farm. Ruth died of Lou Gehrig's disease at age 72.

The five Christian brothers. (Left to right) Ed, Tom, Mike, Ken, and Dave.

I was named after my grandfather Frank and my uncle Frank, who was called "Bubs." Because I interrupted their poker game, my father always said they gave birth to a joker.

I had a very good upbringing. My father was a full-time police officer and a truck farmer, and we had a 160 acres and raised 50 hogs. My father used to say he raised pigs and five kids, in that order. On May 5, 1939, my brother Edward Merlyn came into the world. He was followed by David Howard on February 27, 1942, and then Michael Benjamin on June 27, 1945. We were the five Christian brothers. When our Mother visited California one year, she bought each of us a set of Christian Brothers wineglasses. Our father said he had a secret formula for having all boys. The two other pregnancies had also been male. One day, I heard my father say he was tired of five boys, and maybe they should try for a baseball team. My mother looked at him and said she hoped he would be happy with his second wife.

On our farm truck, we had the name "The Christian Brothers" painted on the side doors for all to see. As we drove off each day to pick up garbage for the pigs, we would often accompany our father to help roll the garbage cans onto the truck. My father invented a hydraulic lift that worked off the truck motor, and it would carry the cans to the truck bed level, and we would roll them to the back of the truck. People said my father should get a patent on it, but he said it worked for him, and he didn't have time for a patent. It did help us have a baseball-size muscle in our arms. We collected garbage from the old soldiers' home, the local navy base, the St. Joseph's Children's Home, and a few other small restaurants in the Minneapolis area. Our pigs ate well. My father often stopped at Storker's Inn for a beer on the way home, and we would have a tall orange drink.

In the Assumption Catholic Church Cemetery in Richfield, Minnesota, we can trace our family on our father's side back four generations. We often walk through the cemetery and visit our history and pay our respects to our ancestors. Our great-grandparents were Peter and Kunnigunda. Peter (1824–1897) came over from Brutig, Trier, Germany, and Kunnigunda Brandt (1829–1899) was from Neuhagen, Trier, Germany. Our grandparents were Frank Christian

(1870–1942) and Theresia Oster. Our parents Edward (1904–1966) and Ruth (1905–1978) and our stillborn brother (he was to be called Edward also) and our brother Mike's ashes round out the four generations. My living brother Ed has the last lot next to our parents, and he plans to be buried there someday. My wife and I have made plans to donate our bodies to the local medical school's Anatomy Bequest Program. Once they are done with us, they will cremate us, and I have requested that my ashes be spread in the Catalina Mountains in Tucson, Arizona, and in Lower Spunk Lake at our summer home in Avon, Minnesota. However, the Arizona program has decided not to give us the ashes but bury them in a respectful place in Tucson. If I pass on in Minnesota, my wishes will be honored; so if I am not feeling well in the future, I may make a quick trip to the "Minneapple" and die happy.

Our father's family had eleven children. I list them now like they do in the Bible, so stay with me because in the course of this book, I will refer to a number of them who interacted with my life over the years. If you are bored, you can skip the next few pages and pick up the narrative in chapter 2.

The Farm

6400 Twelfth Avenue South, Richfield

My father's first sister was named Frances, who married Lester Johnson and moved to La Jolla, California. We would see her periodically, but she always sent us a box of dates at Christmastime. Loved those dates, and they still are one of my favorite fruits. They had no children. When she died, her will had a hundred dollars for me to say Mass for her soul. One of my other aunts said, because I had resigned from the priesthood, I was accepting the money under false pretenses. I did remember her at Mass as a layperson. I do not feel at all guilty. Thank you very much, Aunt Frances.

Next there was Clarence, who married Dagmar Hanson and had four children: Gary, William (Bill), Patricia, and Paul (Skip).

They had a farm close to us, and we always played together and picked potatoes in the fall. My brother Ed and I were crowned potato-picking champions in the area. Clarence became the patriarch of the family after my grandfather passed away in 1942. Our grandfather was one of the first councilmen for the village of Richfield. Uncle Clarence was later the mayor of Richfield and on the board of directors at the Richfield State Bank. Often, at the end of the day picking potatoes, Uncle Clarence would have my cousin Gary and I wrestle after the last bushel of potatoes was loaded. I guess he thought if we were not tired enough, this would take the last part of our energy out of us so we would not be tempted to goof off anymore.

Theodore (Ted), the next family member, married Velva Moore, and they had four children: Barbara (our oldest and smartest cousin), Joan, Nancy, and Mark. They had a farm in Rosemont, and we would visit them often. Mark was my age, so we always had a good time together. Barbara was the president of the National Retired Teachers' Association. Mark died of lung cancer at the age of forty-nine, and Nancy died of Alzheimer's disease at the age of seventy-seven. She was a nurse who today could have been a doctor. She was valedictorian of her high school class. I often wondered how someone so smart could suffer from such a disease. We had family picnics on holidays at Ted and Velva's farm. One time, Uncle Clarence had me run up the hill to the public cemetery in the back of the farm; and because it was dark, he gave me a book of matches to scratch a match on a tombstone and read the name of the deceased and report it back to the group. I did the deed, as I was running back down the hill, my uncle had all the other kids hiding. And as I passed them, they would jump out to scare me. It was all good, clean fun, but I had to admit, I was more than scared. I wasn't ready to volunteer too often after that to show off to my cousins.

My father, Edward, was next in the family line and was followed by Margery, who married Edgar Stromwall, and they lived in Foreston in Central Minnesota. They had three daughters: Marilyn, Jeanne, and Barbara. Margie died of cancer at age forty-two, and the family had to survive without a mother. I remember once wearing a sweatshirt with a hood and pockets in the front. Margie asked me, when I had my hands in the front pockets, if I was pregnant. I must have been about six years old, so I said, "No." She laughed and laughed. I still remember it well.

Donald was next in line in the family, and he married Bernice "Bebe" Larson. Donald was in World War Two. I think the war affected him. He was more quiet than normal when he returned home from the war and worked for the village of Richfield driving a maintenance truck. He died of Parkinson's disease. They had no children.

The next brother was Benjamin, and he married Verna Olson. They had one son, Gregory. Ben was a pilot for Northwest Airlines and flew the original flight to Japan in 1947. Later, he was flying a flight to the Orient and was killed in a plane crash over Edmonton, Alberta, in 1948. He was the pilot, but he had the copilot in training and gave him the controls. But he started to have problems, so Ben took back over. It was too late, and Ben had to make a crash landing. He had all the passengers get in the tail of the plane. He and the copilot were in the cockpit when they landed successfully, but a spare engine in the cargo area broke loose and crushed them. In those days, cargo on the Orient flights were stowed right behind the cockpit. All the crew and passengers were safe. I remember the call with the bad news. It was one of the few times I saw my father cry. He wondered how to tell his sisters. I offered to call them, but at age eleven, he just looked at me and said, "No, you won't." Verna married again, and Greg was adopted by his stepfather, and they moved to Indiana. Greg Server went on to be a member of the Indiana House of Representatives and the Indiana State Senate and was appointed commissioner of the Indiana Utility Regulatory Commission. He finished his career on the Indiana State Parole Board. We would not see him again until our brother Ed organized a Christian family reunion in 2014.

Frank, known as "Bubs," was the youngest brother. He was my godfather. He married Esther "Petie" Peters, and they had one son, Kevin. Bubs was also a pilot for Northwest Airlines. He was on loan to the military, carrying cargo during the Second World War in the Aleutian Islands. He was on automatic instruments when the plane came out of the fog, and there was a mountain. I still remember his funeral. Bubs's brother Ben led the funeral cars to the cemetery on his motorcycle.

When I was five, Godfather Bubs gave me a book on Alaska and the Eskimos. I treasured that book for years. I also remember that he and Ben would fly around our farm. They would use the field in the back of the old Christian family farm as a runway. One day, Bubs landed in the swamp on our farm. We called it mud lake for good reason. With pontoons on the plane, he taxied up to the shore and gave us kids a ride. After he was up and circling our farm, he said, "Oh, oh!" He had shut off the motor, and we were just gliding. He looked at me and said, "What are we going to do now?" I looked at him and smiled. I said, "You are the pilot." He laughed heartily, smiled at me, and then turned back on the motor, and we kept on flying and came in for a safe landing. He later told the story and said how cool I was at the time.

I later saw the letter Bub's family received called the Citation for Air Medal given posthumously from President Harry Truman. It read, "Frank J. Christian, civilian pilot of Northwest Air Lines. For meritorious achievement while participating in aerial flights between September 1942 and December 1944. Mr. Christian flew, both as pilot and co-pilot, a total of 1326 hours in the Northern Region and 521 hours in the Aleutian area. His splendid example inspired all who associated with him."

With two uncles killed in plane crashes, it would not be the end of our plane tragedies. My brother Ken and his wife, Ellie, would lose their thirty-year-old son Nick to another plane accident on September 10, 1996. Jonathon Nicholas was flying skydivers and was on his tenth and last trip of the day when one of his engines went out. He had landed planes before with one engine, so he calmly proceeded to bank the plane and prepare for a landing. It appears that one of the eleven passengers was also a pilot, and he decided to jump out on his own when he saw they were in trouble. He stepped to the cargo opening with his parachute on and, apparently being a big man and overweight, tipped the plane enough to cause it to tailspin. Nick could not pull it out, and it crashed into a house. Eleven passengers were killed, including Nick and a gentleman who was sitting on his porch reading his Bible. Ten of the skydivers were in their seat belts, and the one who was trying to parachute out on his own was found loose by the cargo door. The verdict on the crash was pilot error. I do not fear flying, but I do not go up anymore in small planes for a joyride.

Our father's second sister was Leonida, whom we always called Neda. Neda never married. She had a couple of opportunities too, but one was cut short when her boyfriend was killed in a car accident. The other person she wanted to marry didn't meet her brother Clarence's expectations. Neda became a caretaker for her mother and the neighboring bachelor farmer Joe Alt and a second mother to her sister Theresa's five daughters. She would suffer from depression problems for the rest of her life. At one of our cousin's wedding, Neda told me I was not in her will. She decided to give her money to our cousins who had lost a parent as they were growing up. It seemed to be a good idea. She had also inherited the farm from her neighbor Joe Alt, so she had some money to give away.

Madonna, the third sister, married Ralph Mangan. They had two children: Maria and Ralph Jr. They went on to celebrate their fiftieth wedding anniversary at one of our Christian family reunions.

The youngest sister, Theresa, married Gerard "Bud" Boeser, and they had five daughters: Jennifer, Sally, Mary, Bonnie, and Rita. Theresa died in 2007.

My great-grandparents Peter and Kunnigunda had seven children. Henry married Mary Tully, and they had eleven children. Katherine (Kate) married Albert Pahl, and they had nine children. Charles married Mary Haeg, and they had eight children. My grandfather Frank married Theresia Oster, and they had eleven children. Peter married Mina Libert, and they had three children. Caroline married John Haeg and bore him eleven children. Elizabeth married Edward Yetzer, and they had five children. You can see how we are related to many of the families in the Richfield and Bloomington area.

Our mother was the first of five born to William and Ernestine Carney. William was born in Iowa and was a cattle buyer. He was also a deputy federal marshal and died from wounds suffered in the line of duty. The family lived in Bird Island, Minnesota. The local bank was robbed, and the marshal and his deputies had the desperadoes cornered in a corral filled with a herd of wild horses. The robbers opened the gate and rode the horses out in an attempt to escape. My grandfather was pinned against the railroad car, and the sliding door came down on him. He was crushed by the weight of the doors. He lived for a few months lying on the living-room couch. That is what they did in 1918. The death certificate stated he died of tuberculous of the hip. Our mother, born September 29, 1905, was thirteen at the time and in her first year of high school. The family then moved to Minneapolis, and she took a job and worked her way up to book-keeper at Munsingware clothing factory. She had to do her part to support her family.

Our mother's four brothers had difficult lives. George, born on March 23, 1912, died of chronic cardiac decompensation on February 5, 1924, at the age of eleven and ten months.

Leland born August 17, 1902, married Anne, and had two boys and a girl: William, Dale, and Darlene. He died on January19, 1957. I was a sophomore in college at Saint John's University in Collegeville, Minnesota. We were in Northfield, Minnesota, at Carlton College. I was on the Minnesota Intercollegiate Athletic Conference (MIAC) state championship wrestling team and just came off the mat when I was informed that a member of my family had died. I ran to the phone thinking it was my dad. He had asthma, and I would see him go outside gasping for air as he got ready to go on the police car or working on the farm. Maybe he had been killed like one of his old partners Freddy Babcock. Freddy had been shot in a burglary of a National Tea store in Richfield. Freddy first dropped off his part-ner Lee Poulter at the back of the store to catch the perpetrators if they came out the back doors. Freddy then drove through the alley and stopped a short distance from the front of the store. He was getting out of the squad car, holding the door as a shield. It was dark and after hours, so he didn't see the lookout man hiding across the street. He was shot and was dead on arrival at the hospital. He had switched that shift with another officer who wanted the time off. The four suspects were caught. Gustav Johnson, twenty-nine, was apprehended a couple of miles from the scene with the help of bloodhounds. The other three—Arthur E. Bistrom, thirty-seven; his brother Carl H., twenty-seven; and Allen C. Hartman, twenty-six— all from St. Paul, were taken into custody after what the Minneapolis Police Department called the most intense manhunt in twenty years. The Richfield Police Department held a benefit for Freddy's family, and the Ink Spots gave a free performance. I always loved the Ink Spots from that day onward.

Back to the wrestling mat, I called from the public phone in the hallway at the school. I held my breath when my mother told me it was our uncle Lee who had died. I felt guilty being somewhat relieved.

My mother's next brother was Merlyn, born November 6, 1907. He married Emma Josephine, whom we called "Jo," and they had two boys: James and Robert. Merlyn had chicken pox when he was young, and one of the pox developed on his eyeball, and he was blind in that eye. I remember as a five-year-old being in the bathtub on our farm when Merlyn came in to use the facilities. He was visiting us but was so intoxicated that he fell by the toilet bowl. He got up and used the sink to relieve himself. He turned to me in the tub, and he said don't tell anybody what he did. I was five at the time, and this is the first time I have mentioned it. Years later, Merlyn died of alcoholism on April 8, 1955. He actually suffocated on his own vomit and was found with his head in the chamber pot. His brother Lee found him and announced to his mother, "There is a stiff in there."

I still remember at the cemetery the priest had been told that Lee also had an alcohol problem, and I heard him warn Lee that he would end up like Merlyn if he didn't change his ways. It didn't work because Lee also was divorced due to his drinking and died of arteriosclerotic heart disease caused by alcoholism less than two years after Merlyn. In those days, people did not see alcoholism as a disease and addiction. It was seen as a weakness and little willpower.

Merlyn and Jo's two sons had tough childhoods. After Merlyn died, Jo had to support the family. She was an excellent cook. Being Bohemian, she made the best kolaches in the world. She had to put her two boys in the local Saint Joseph's Children's Home for a while. When we lived on the farm, one of our stops, as I said, was the children's home to pick up garbage for the pigs. We didn't know we had two of our first cousins boarding there. One of the boys got himself in trouble with the law when he and a friend were burglarizing a bar after hours. The owner lived upstairs and heard the break-in. He came down the stairs with his gun. One of the burglars ran out of the building crouched over to avoid being a target. The proprietor shot low at the moving shadow. He said he was trying to hit him in the leg. The bullet entered the young man's neck, and he died at the scene. In the meantime, the other perpetrator got away. The police were called, and both Minneapolis and Richfield police arrived. Our father was on duty. Being experienced, he told his partner to help him check the parked cars in the area. All of a sudden, our father walked across the street to his partner and said, "He is hiding on the floor in the back of the third car over there. You make the arrest, and I will cover you from the shadows. It's my nephew and my godson, and I don't want him to see me."

Our cousin did time in the Saint Cloud Reformatory. Until he reads this, he never knew that his uncle and godfather was one of the police officers responsible for his arrest.

Our same cousin had another run-in with the law. This time, he was in Mexico buying some dope to sell to his friends back in Las Vegas, Nevada. He did not make his buy yet when he picked up a hitchhiker to give him a ride. He didn't realize that the hitchhiker was under surveillance by the Mexican police. They followed him after he let the young man off. As he entered his motel room, they came in right behind him. They found a small amount of marijuana he had for his personal use. He saw it on his dresser in a bag, and as the federal police looked around his room, he slowly pushed the envelope onto the floor. He planned to stand on it and avoid detection. It didn't work. They spotted it, and he was under arrest. They saw him as a big drug dealer and wanted to know whom he worked for and what his connections were. He could not convince them. They put the gun to his head and pulled the trigger. It was an empty gun. He was convicted of possession and would serve seven years on a ten-year sentence in a Mexican prison. Later, as I worked in corrections, I was able to get him an attorney, and we got him transferred to a halfway house in Minneapolis. There was an exchange program between Mexico and the United States. As a prisoner, he had lost his hair, and his teeth rotted while he was in prison. Needless to say, he has pretty much stayed out of trouble since that experience. As he told me the story, I said we could write his own book on his many experiences.

Chester, our mother's youngest brother, also was an alcoholic. His nickname was "Jeff," and his brother Merlyn was called "Mutt" after the comic duo in the paper. Chester wanted to be called Chet or Chester once he sobered up for good. After his brother Merlyn died, he said if there is no more "Mutt," then there is no more "Jeff."

One day, he was in downtown Minneapolis and walked into a diner. He sat down next to a trucker and asked him what he had as his load. The driver made the mistake of saying he had whiskey on board. Chester drank his coffee and got up and went out and popped the ignition and drove off with the truck. He went down the street three blocks and pulled into an alley. The police found him in the front seat drinking a quart of whiskey. He was sentenced to eight years in Stillwater Prison in Minnesota. I remember reading a letter from him when he was getting out asking our father to get him a job so it would look better at his parole hearing.

Chester did get into Alcoholics Anonymous and started working doing twelve-step work at a treatment center called Pine Manor in Pine City, Minnesota. He had a few slips along the way, but he eventually bought the program, and he was sober until he passed away at the age of seventy-five. He told me that he had been a cowboy in Montana and was married once. He was drunk and woke up in bed with a lady he didn't know. When she told him they had been married the night before, he was surprised. Needless to say, the marriage was annulled. After his death, another lady came forward who said she was a good friend of Chester. He had an interesting life.

Chester developed diabetes and eventually had both his legs amputated. He walked with two artificial limbs and proceeded to help many other people with their addictions. He found his calling working with fellow drunks.

On his deathbed, Chester announced he was "at the end of his rope," and then he died. Our good friend Father Ray Monsour visited with him on his deathbed.

Our grandmother on our mother's side was Ernestine Buss born July 17, 1881. They all called her "Tina." She lived in an apartment down on Chicago Avenue and Fourteenth in Minneapolis. As kids, we used to visit her with our parents. It was a small, modest apartment with dark hallways. It was a rough part of town. Beanies and Danny's Bars were nearby, and many times we would end up there to have an orange drink while we visited Grandma Carney. We usually found her in the bar. She carried a jar in her purse, and when people bought her a drink, she often poured most of the drink in the jar. She was then available for the next round. At the end of the evening, she would bring the jar to her apartment and have a nightcap. She would always wink at us when she played her jar trick.

When Grandma visited us, she used to sit in the bathroom, and we could hear her pass gas. We always thought she had the record for the longest farts. One day, our brother Dave heard the bathroom noise, and he said, "Grandma's here." It wasn't Grandma. She was still downtown. It was my father this time. We all had a good laugh on my brother, and even my mother got a chuckle.

One story I heard on Grandma Tina involved an old boyfriend whom she knew long after my grandfather had died. When Grandma told him she wanted out of the relationship, he shot himself in front of Grandma Tina. The story was that it did not faze her at all. She just walked out of the room. She had another boyfriend named Cecil. He was a friendly sort and laughed a lot. After my father passed away, Tina came to live with my mother. Grandma often screened my mother's telephone calls, and if it was a potential boyfriend for my mother, she would say my mother was not at home. Often, when I came home to visit, Tina would slip me a five-dollar bill and ask me to get her a jug of Christian Brothers brandy. Years before on a doctor's visit for a physical, she was asked if she used alcohol. She said she had a shot of brandy before she went to bed. The doctor told her it was good for her circulation, and she should have a drink after every meal. She liked that doctor and followed his advice to the letter until she died.

One day, Tina was ill, and it looked like she was dying. She told our mother to call our sister-in-law Ellen. Ellie did hair, and Tina said if she died, she wanted to look halfway decent. Ellie came over, and Tina got up from her deathbed and made it to the kitchen sink and had her hair washed and set. She then crawled back into her bed and died the next day, March 21, 1969, at the age of eighty-eight.

You can't ask for a better upbringing than we had on the farm. We had 160 acres to roam about, ride horses, and explore the nearby swamp, the woodlands, and the fields. We raised pigs and chickens, had a cow, and over the years, four horses. We had our own pony called Muttsie. We got him when the Richfield chief of police Cy Johnson bought a Shetland pony and a small stagecoach for his granddaughter. She didn't like it. Our father said he would buy it for his five children. The timing was right, and we were in business. We would give rides to the neighbor kids and all our friends and cousins. We had a great time. One of us would steer the stagecoach full of guests, and the other brother would ride one of the other horses, put on a handkerchief over his mouth, and hold up the stagecoach. A fake fight would ensue, and one of us would knock the other down, and he would roll off the stagecoach under the wheels. The wheels were car tires filled with air, so it would not hurt us as we got run over. We made one mistake, though, and thought the stagecoach looked too fancy and a buckboard would be cooler. We stripped the stagecoach down to the bare buckboard. Looking back, that was not a good idea, but we made the best of it.

Our other horses were Queen and Flying Heels. We also boarded an Arabian mare named Princess. Queen was for my oldest brother, Ken, and Ed and I rode Muttsie and Flying Heels. One day, Ken and the neighbor kid Richard Bloom were riding double on the new Arabian mare. I followed on Flying Heels. All of a sudden, the Arabian was spooked and took off across the potato field. Ken and Richard were hanging on for dear life. I rode behind watching the whole show. As they headed for the highway, I saw a car coming, and they were heading right for it. It was like a movie. I guess the driver thought they were going to stop. They didn't. The car crashed into the horse, and Ken and Richard went flying. The car hit Ken with the bumper and broke his leg in two places. It was a compound fracture. The driver didn't know what to do. I was standing over them with Flying Heels in one hand and the Arabian mare in the other. Ken was on the ground, and Richard was knocked out in the ditch. Ken said he lived on the farm a mile down the road and wanted to go home. Much to our parents' dismay, the driver picked him up and put him in the front seat of his automobile and drove him to the farm. I followed riding Flying Heels and leading the Arabian. Our father was on the squad car, so he raced to the scene. They hauled my brother to the hospital, and I took the horses back to the corral and put salve on the Arabian's leg where he had been cut. Our dad's partner George Brening asked me what happened and was filling out a report. When I told him about Richard Bloom being on the horse too, he said, "Where is Richard now?"

I said, "He is still there, lying in the ditch."

They hurried back to the scene of the accident, and there was Richard Bloom, still unconscious. Richard was okay, but my brother Ken had his leg up in the air with a cast in the hospital until it started to heal correctly. He had a roommate who liked to swing Ken's leg when he went by. The leg was up in a sling. Not only was it painful, but it did not help the healing process either.

Brother Ed also had an episode on Muttsie. He was riding double with a neighbor by the name of Donny Bobendrier. They were riding bareback as we often did. Donny started to fall off, and he pulled my brother Ed down with him. The horse stepped on Ed's arm, and we had another compound fracture. Ed walked into the farmhouse, and our mother was on the phone talking to our aunt Neda. "Don't bother me now, Edward. Can't you see I am on the phone talking to your aunt Neda?"

"I think I broke my arm," Ed said as he showed her the bone sticking out of the skin.

"Oh my God, Edward broke his arm. I am going to have to call Hattie (a nickname they called my father because, at parties, he would always go into the hall closet wherever he was and come out wearing a different hat)." Our mother hung up on Neda and called the cops again. This time, it was on Edward. We all signed Ed's cast, but he continued to ride Muttsie like nothing much happened.

We always had dogs on the farm. As a police officer, our father found many stray dogs running loose. We never had more than two dogs at one time and no cats. We had some wildcats around, which we called civet cats.

I was bitten twice by two different dogs, and I still can show you the scars. The first was Max. We were walking down the dirt road to the farmhouse when I saw his tail wagging. Being only four years old, I thought it looked like something to grab a hold of. Max didn't think so. He turned and bit me on the nose. No plastic surgery in those days. Nobody held it against Max when they heard my story.

The second bite was from "Puppy." We had two dogs, and this time, we couldn't decide on a name for the second one. So because he was a little pup, we just called him Puppy. On the farm, we fed the pigs garbage from a number of places in the city. This was good for the pigs, but it attracted rats and a smell that eventually got the neighbors over a mile away to our east a little upset. One of our dogs was a rat terrier, and he was great at keeping the rat population down. He also taught Puppy how to hunt rats. Puppy had to be tied up when we had company because he bit a neighbor kid's ear one day. Earlier in his career, he had been in a pen when another neighbor kid came over with his BB gun. Before we spotted him, he had shot Puppy a number of times in the rear end as a joke. In the pen, Puppy had no place to hide. When we left him out, he was always leery of strange kids. One day, while we had visitors, we saw a rat in the grain bin. It was time to show off to our young guests how Puppy could catch a rat. I untied him and led him to the grain bin. My young friends followed. Within minutes, Puppy had the rat and shook him to his death. Now it was time to hook Puppy up to his chain. He didn't think so. After all that good work, he didn't deserve this.

As I grabbed his collar, he turned and bit my wrist. I ran to the ladder in the grain bin and started up with Puppy still hanging on to my wrist. About halfway up the ladder, he let go. Puppy didn't get tied up the rest of that day.

One of the sad stories about Puppy happened next. Our father came out one day and found a pig had been killed in the pigpen up against a wall by the feeding troughs. It looked like the work of a dog. That night, our father and his partner on the police car, George Brening, made their normal rounds. Our father saw another pig by the wall and the troughs. Puppy was there barking. Our dad turned to George and said, "He is the kids' favorite, but if he is a pig killer, we have to shoot him."

George got out of the car. Puppy, knowing him, came up to him to be petted. George put one shot in him. At the sound of the shot, a pack of dogs came around the wall and started running. Puppy had been protecting the pig from the pack of dogs. This is another reason I am against the death penalty. Our father felt terrible, and he said to George, "Let's go!" They took the squad car and followed the pack of dogs and began shooting them as they drove down the road. No dog was left standing. We never heard from the neighbors about any missing dogs. They must have been hit by cars was the only conclusion.

We used to pick potatoes on the farm for our uncle Clarence. We would get a nickel a bushel. This would give us enough money to go to the Saturday afternoon movies. It was twelve cents to see the movie back then. Each week, we would see a movie and the serial that left the hero hanging from a cliff, so we had to go back and see the next episode the following week. The hero always survived.

Our mother would drive us to the Parkway Theater, which was in Minneapolis. We had some problems with the car on occasion. Our father used to buy the old police cars at a good discount. One of the cars had a passenger door that would come off, so we would all have to get in the back seat. One day, as our mother dropped us off at the movie and as we were standing in line for tickets, we saw our mother pull up alongside the streetcar. The streetcar opened its door and snagged our side door. Off came the door again. As our mother was talking to the streetcar conductor, I stepped out of line and went over to her and said, "Did that darn door come off again?"

Our mother looked at me like, *Nice going.* They put the door on again, and Mom drove off. Fortunately, our mother and father had a good sense of humor as they told that story for the next few days. But the door finally got fixed.

When we finished picking the potato crop for our uncle during the week, we would go to neighboring farms and pick for them. My brother Ed and I would get into races to see who could pick the fastest. We would start at the beginning of a row and pick to the end of it. We worked as a team. We would fill the bushel basket and then dump it in a gunnysack. Ed and I were quick, so we were declared potato-picking champions. Little did we know that we were making more money for the farmers by picking so fast.

One of our cousins only had a daughter, so he hired Ed and I to do a number of other chores. We were paid fifty cents an hour. Another friend of ours from school, Bob McGinn, wanted to get in on the act. Our cousin said he couldn't pay us more than a dollar an hour for the two of us. If a third person came with the package, he could only pay us thirty-three cents an hour a piece. In those days, it was more important to have fun while we worked, so we took the deal.

Our cousins were good potato pickers too, so the challenge was made. Two women could outpick the Christian brothers. Ed and I looked at each other and said, "No way, Jose." The race was on. Ed and I could pick up the sacks and dump the potato bushel basket quicker than our rivals. We smoked them. We picked so fast we got out early that day.

We had an old tin tub that we took baths in when the weather in Minnesota permitted. Uncle Chester used to call us three men in a tub when Ken, Ed, and I took baths together. He called my younger brother Ed "Rub a Dub."

One day, we had the bright idea to take the tub next door to Mud Lake (actually a swamp) and play Tom Sawyer and Huck Finn. Our parents were up by the house, so they didn't see us carry it down. We sat in the tub and paddled around. Some of the neighbor kids were swimming with us and, coming up, would hang on to the tub. I was four and didn't know how to swim well yet. I stood on the edge of the tub and looked over watching Ken and the others. Guy Bobendrier came up to the tub and grabbed the side. I flipped out like a cork. The swamp water was murky, and I sank down into the abyss. I kept my eyes open and my mouth closed. I saw Guy swim down to me and try to pull me up. Not knowing I was in trouble, I kept avoiding his grasp. Finally, he got a hold of me and pulled me to the surface. Another adventure we didn't tell our parents about. The tub sank, and our father asked where it was, and we said we didn't know. He had to find another tub to mix his cement in.

The next scary event in my life involved brother Ken and our neighbor Guy again. Our parents were gone, and they hired a babysitter. She was on the phone with her boyfriend the minute our parents left the house.

Ken and Guy went to the kitchen and pulled a chair up to the closet. One chair was not enough to reach the cubbyhole above the closet. They put the chair on top of the table. They now could get into the cubbyhole. That was where our dad kept his police revolver, a .38 special. His belt with the bullets came sliding down with them. Ken loaded the gun, six shots, and they came outside. There I was, standing about ten feet from them in the yard. Ken aimed the gun right at me, looked at Guy, and they both laughed. And then he fired. The kick from the gun caused the gun to drop, and I saw a tomato-can cover bounce at my feet. They laughed again and moved on. They walked down the road a mile to the plot of homes, shooting at things as they went. They saw one of the other kids that they didn't like that much. Guy said, "Should we shoot him or put my Dick Tracy handcuffs on him?"

Fortunately, they wanted to try out the handcuffs and save the last bullet. Soon out of bullets, they returned to the farmhouse and tried to put the gun in the cubbyhole. They could put the holster in by throwing it, but the gun they couldn't get back. They left it on the kitchen table. Our father was not too happy. He bought a small safe with a lock and key, and the gun never was within reach again. Ken and I have often thought what would have happened if he had hit me with the gun or even taken me out. Ken went on to a distinguished career in the criminal justice field as a police officer, state crime investigator, and a professor of security at Michigan State University School of Criminal Justice. He could have ended up in a correctional facility for delinquents. Gun control and gun safety are high on both our priorities.

We did a few other dangerous things back on the farm, including climbing to top of the windmill. After we came down one time, our father was waiting for us. Ed and I compared red hind ends after that one.

Ken had another adventure when he lassoed the cow in the pasture to show off for the neighbor kids. The cow pulled away, but the rope was too tight, and it choked to death. Our father had to call in the rendering plant to take away the cow to be used to make soap.

We had two fires on the farm and one incident where a blowtorch blew the windows out of the farmhouse. The first mysterious fire involved the haystack next to the barn. It was about twenty feet high and was used to feed the horses and cow. One day, it started on fire, and we thought the barn and all would go up. We blamed it on the neighbor kids, but overtime, my brother Ken admitted that he and same old neighbor Guy were playing with matches, and the fire got away from them. It burned for hours, and the smoke and burning hay covered the farmyard so you couldn't see. We kids helped keep it from getting as far as the barn and other outbuildings by hauling pails of water to stop it from spreading.

The second fire involved the whole pasture. Again, the fire raged out of control, and we watched it burn up most of the grass available to feed the horses and cow. It was also blamed on the neighborhood kids. Years later, after we moved off the farm, I noticed my brother Ed had an A on an English assignment. Now, Ed was an A student, so I was not surprised. Out of curiosity, I picked up the paper and read the story. It was about the fire in the pasture. He admitted that he was playing with matches, and a small fire got out of hand. And before he knew it, the whole pasture was up in flames. He never dared to tell our father. Ed as an adult joined the Bloomington Fire Department. It was an all-volunteer outfit, and Ed worked his way up to be deputy chief. Ken was also on the fire department, so I guess they got their share of fires to put out.

The third incident was our father's doing. It was a cold Minnesota winter, and the pipes in the dirt basement cellar of the house froze up. He had a blowtorch and was running it on the pipes in the basement. This included the hot-water heater too. After a period of time, he had to get ready to go to work on the police squad car. He decided to let the blowtorch run on its own while he went upstairs and put on his uniform. All of a sudden, the whole thing blew up. All the windows on the first floor blew out, and the floorboards in the bedroom tore up. The furniture was pushed all around, and the bedspread ended up on the dresser mirror. No one was hurt, but it was like a bomb had gone off. We helped our dad replace all the windows.

Having four brothers, you would think we would have our share of fights. Our father stopped any disagreements in a hurry. He always said, "That is your brother, and you don't hit your brother."

He bought us a speed punching bag and installed it in the basement. He said, "If you want to hit someone, go down in the basement and hit the boxing bag." I became very efficient at hitting that bag.

In fact, I took up boxing at an early age. I would have thirty-one amateur boxing fights in my career. I always said I would be a boxer in the future if I was big enough, and I would be a jockey if I was too small. I started out as a flea weight (97 pounds) and had my last fight as a light heavyweight (175 pounds).

I was never knocked out or knocked down, but a lady named Mae Anderson did the job when I was only five. Mae used to come to visit our parents on occasion, and when she left, we used to run up and stand on the back bumper of her old car as she drove down our dirt road to the main Sixty-Sixth street. We hid down so she couldn't see us, and then we would jump off and lose our balance and go falling into the ditch. One time, I held on too long, and she got going too fast, so when I jumped, I hit my head on the ground, and—you guessed it—I was knocked out cold. I woke up in bed with my parents looking over me. I was okay, but the rides on Mae Anderson's car came to a screeching halt.

Another character who came to the farm to do plumbing work was an old German named Nick Schmidt. He was an old-time wrestler, and he used to fight in the local tavern called the Frenchman's. He would take on anybody, and people would bet and then pass the hat for Nick. His house was about two miles away from us, and it looked like the local dump, inside and out. But if you ever needed anything fixed, Nick had the part somewhere in his yard, and he was the man to call. He used to wrestle with us, and he had the greatest laugh you ever heard. He had cauliflower ears and was a small bear. Later, as I wrestled in college, I would remember old Nick.

When one of the neighboring farmers died, our father was at the funeral, and the widow didn't know what she would do. Our father offered to buy the farm with his brother Clarence, and arrangements were made for the sale. After the deal was finalized, one of the widow's cousins came back to our father and said he and his brother wanted to buy the farm back and keep it in their family. Their aunt had moved to sell too fast. In those days, it was not a big deal, and our father sold it back to them at the same price. The land is now the Mall of America, the biggest mall in the United States. Yes, we owned it for about two weeks, but would we have been happy with all that money? We would never know.

One day, we got the bright idea of creating Jesse James's grave. We went out into the pasture into a wooded area. We dug a grave and placed pig bones in the shape of a human body. We then covered it up. It was only about two feet down, and we would bring kids out when we had company and tell them about Jesse James's grave. Then we would dig up the bones and prove it to them.

We had great times on the farm.

We had a pig farm, so we needed to feed the pigs each day. As I had mentioned, our father had an arrangement with a number of places to pick up their garbage.

We often found items in the garbage cans that we could use. At the navy base, we found silverware all the time. We all ended up with a set of silverware. With the letters *USN* on them, they became more valuable as time went on. When our mother moved out of her house in Richfield years later, she had a bushel basket full of navy silverware. An antique dealer told us how valuable they really were.

One day at the navy base, we found a couple of flight jackets in the garbage. We had them cleaned up and promised our mother we would never tell anyone where we had gotten them. She scared us by saying the government would come after us if they found out.

One day, our father was on the police squad car, and he pulled into Yetzer's auto garage. Lyle Yetzer was sitting in his car with his friends and called over to our dad. Lyle was a jokester, so he told his friends, "Watch this."

He had his car wired, so if you touched the metal, one would get a shock. Our dad was a friendly guy, so here he came in his police uniform, and he put his arm on top of Lyle's car and asked what was happening. Lyle hit the switch, and our dad jumped away from the shock. Lyle and his friends had a great laugh at out father's expense.

A couple of days later, our father pulled into the same auto garage. This time, he had the garbage truck. Sure enough, Lyle was there with his friends again, sitting in his hot car. Our father stepped out of his truck, but this time, he pulled the electric prod gun used to get the pigs to go up the ramp into the truck to be hauled to market. He slowly walked over to Lyle's car. He had the battery loaded, prod hiding alongside his leg. As he approached the car, he pulled out the prod and got Lyle in the front seat. Lyle was behind the steering wheel, so he couldn't move. Our dad stuck him a few times and gave him a good shock. Our dad had the last laugh. Today, if someone did that, there might be a lawsuit. Lyle's dad thought it served him right.

One other time, our dad was in uniform and stopped in a local gas station to go to the bathroom. Another wise guy decided to throw a cheery bomb through the open window at the top of the bathroom door. It went off, and as our dad came out, everybody was laughing again. They pulled a trick on the police officer. He said everyone sounded like Donald Duck for days, but his hearing was affected for the rest of his life.

We used to have chicken every Sunday. At least we thought it was chicken. As we got older, we would be working with our dad; and all of a sudden, he would pull his shotgun out from behind the seat in the truck. *Bang!* Down would go a pheasant. That Sunday, we had "chicken" again. Being a police officer, he could not shoot pheasants out of season. He told us he fed the pheasants along with the pigs, so he felt he could shoot one pheasant once in a while. When we got older, he told us to keep saying we had chicken every Sunday.

One day, our dad shot a bevy of pheasants with one shot. They were sticking their heads out of a clump of weeds, and when he pulled the trigger, six pheasants went down. Of course, it was out of season, so he had to wait until pheasant season was open before he could tell anybody that he got six pheasants with one shot.

Assumption Church and School

Richfield

When we were on the farm, we attended Assumption Church and School. This was an old German community, and the priest who came in November of 1916 was Father Peter Schmitz (no relation, believe me, to Nick Schmidt). The nuns were Benedictine Sisters of St. Joseph, and they first came to the parish in 1900. They wore the old habits with the long black robes and the head covering with the rosary around their waists and the white wimple under their chins. When we started school in 1941, Sister Mary Werner was the first-grade teacher, and Sister Theodora was the principal. We did not have kindergarten back in those days, and I started school when I was five years old.

Our father told stories about how the farmers would hitch up their team of horses and go to meet the archbishop at the Mendota Bridge to lead him into the parish for confirmation. Our great-grand-father Peter and great-grandmother Kunnigunda Christian were the first ones married in the Assumption Church.

Easter was the major feast at our church. Christmas was second. The resurrection gave us all hope that when this life was over, we would have a new life in heaven. Even to this day, we do not send out Christmas cards to our relatives and friends. Instead, we send an Easter letter with pictures on one side and our news on the other. We found that people would read our Easter letter because it was usually the only letter like that they would get, and we tried to make it not too boring like some of the Christmas letters we got.

One Easter, I was in first grade and was chosen to be one of the page boys in the Easter vigil. I was all dressed up in tights and a blousey shirt with a big bow tie. I was too young, so I thought it was a real honor. My family and relatives were all proud of me. It may have been a precursor of things to come.

In first grade, Sister Werner had a whip called the cat of nine tails. It hung over the cloakroom door, and when we looked back, we could see it menacingly waiting. She warned us about it, but we never saw her use it. The threat was all she needed.

We did not have inside bathrooms back in 1943. There was a row of outside toilets up on the hill beyond the playground. There were six of them, so you didn't have to wait too often. It was fun to be in class when a kid would ask to go to the bathroom. We could look out our window and see her or him running across the playground and up the hill to the outhouse. We would look at one another and smile, knowing that everybody would be watching us do the same thing when we had to go.

My brother Ed was in first grade when I was in the third year and Ken in his fifth year. They called Ed "Smiley" because he hardly spoke when adults were around. People would give him a quarter because he was so nice and quiet all the time. When Ed hit first grade, his world would change. I always spoke for Ed or translated what he was trying to say.

For example, if you asked him his name, he would say, "Elwood Tushan," instead of "Edward Christian." That was not going to work with Sister Werner and the principal Sister Theodora. When Sister Werner could not get Ed to say his name correctly, even with the threat of the cat of nine tails, she sent him to the principal's office. Sister Theodora did not have much better luck. She finally hung a big sign around Ed's neck that read, "My name is Edward Christian." It didn't take Ed long to tire of that routine, and he told me he was heading home. Now, home was on the farm about three miles away on busy roads. At six years old, that was not a good idea. Ed knew the way because we went to church at Assumption Church every Sunday, but there was no school bus; and we were driven to Assumption School every weekday, so he had certain road signs to keep him on track.

As he walked into the farmyard, our mother came running out, screaming, "Edward, why are you here and not in school?"

Ed told her he was embarrassed and, "I ain't never going to school again." Obviously, that didn't work, and our parents brought Ed back to school, only to be told by Sister Theodora that Edward could not come back to school until he had speech lessons and could talk like other children his age.

We went each week to speech lessons on Saturday. My brother Dave would go along, and he and I would sit and wait for Ed to finish. One day, Dave had to go to the bathroom, so he tried to let our mother know. But she didn't get the picture and told us to wait in the car, and they would soon be done.

Dave proceeded to step out on the steps and do his business in full view of all the people passing by. That was the way we did it on the farm. We called it the fountain of youth. Dave and I stayed home after that.

Ed, of course, learned how to talk; and as we say now, he is a lawyer, and we can't shut him up. He often serves as the master of ceremonies at local events.

Saint Peter's Church and School

Richfield

When I was finishing third grade at the Assumption School, a new parish was formed in Richfield. It was on Sixty-Seventh and Nicollet, and our farm fell into their territory. So off we went to Saint Peter's Church and School. My brother Ken was now in sixth grade, and I was in fourth grade. Brother Ed gladly left first grade and had a new start in second grade. Ken's class would be the first eighth grade graduating class because they started with first to sixth grade.

Saint Peter's was a lot of fun. The pastor was Father William A. Brand, and he was much more personable than old Father Peter

Schmitz at Assumption. Father Brand had worked at Saint Joseph's Children's Home and had a great rapport with kids. He would be one of the main influences for us to go to the seminary. He would come into our classroom and have us recite the Latin prayers to qualify as an altar boy. If we were right, he would flip us a fifty-cent piece. I served Mass from sixth grade through eighth grade.

We had great sports teams at Saint Peter's. Our major teams were in baseball and basketball. We were always one of the top teams in the area. Our class had outstanding talent. Guys like Dale Kaiser, Tom Reifenberger, and Bob McGinn were our core talent. My brother Ed was good enough to make our teams when he was only in the sixth grade.

Tom Reifenberger and I skipped school one day and got caught. Years later, he would marry my brother Mike's first wife, Jeri, and we would strike up our old friendship and golf and party as we became senior citizens.

Football was in the park board leagues. I was fast, and having played with my brothers Ken and Ed, I could run and catch the ball without any problem. They had midget football in the city of Minneapolis and a suburban league for Richfield and surrounding suburbs. My potato-picking cousin Gary Christian was very strong and had no fear. He would block for me, and I would be off to the races. I was chosen all-city and all-suburban in the midget leagues. I was looked at by the coaches at Washburn High School, but I would be going to De LaSalle Catholic High School, I thought.

Boxing was also a big sport in our growing up. I would work out at the local fire barn under the watchful eye of my coach and trainer Lloyd Neiver. I started out at the age of eight fighting as a flea weight, and I would end up at the age of twenty-five as a light heavyweight. My record would be 28–3. I used to run to practice from the farm to the fire barn, so my wind and endurance were excellent. We worked on the farm, so our arm muscle was better than the average kids.

I lost one of my fights in the junior golden gloves to a kid named Nick Torres. I danced around the first round because I had never fought a Mexican before. Once I settled down, I thought I won the next two rounds. I knocked him down, but he was the up-and-coming fighter, and I was in the seminary by then. He was to appear on television the next week, so he got the hometown decision. He went on to turn professional, but I heard he did not get too far in the boxing world. My brother Ed sent me an obituary in 2015, and it was Nick Torres. There was a nice list of his family, so he must have gotten himself together and had a good life.

My second loss was to Michael Novack. I lost points when I held him by the back of the head and hammered him. They gave him that decision too. I thought I had won it, but points were taken away from me for my street fighting. This time, the crowd was on my side, and they booed the decision and threw paper in the ring. The third loss was against Jimmy Osanick. I was able to hit him at ease, but he countered with left and right hooks that had me seeing stars. It hurt that night to put my head on the pillow. He definitely beat me. He went on to become a navy boxing champion.

I beat a guy named Willie in a first-round knockout in a junior golden gloves fight. I met him in the shower afterward, and he said he didn't remember whom he fought. I told him he had fought me, and I was lucky to catch him with a good right hand. Years later, when I was a probation officer, I was assigned a kid with the same name as Willie. I asked him if he had a relative named Willie. He said that was his uncle. I told him to tell his uncle that his probation officer was Tom Christian. The next week, he came in and said his uncle told him he better shape up because Tom Christian took his uncle's head off in the boxing ring years ago.

One other fight I like to brag about is against Irish Tom Collins. Tom Collins was a light heavyweight and was being groomed for the Upper Midwest Golden Gloves. He wanted a tune-up fight, and I was on Christmas vacation from the seminary and available. Tom was a left-hander, and I loved to fight left-handers. I could set them up with my left jab and then come across with a straight right hand. The fight went according to my plan. I hit him hard and often and rocked him with my right hand. I won the fight, and Tom's girlfriend was not a happy camper because I cut him up, and he had a black eye. He was not the pretty boy anymore.

My brother Ed was working slinging pizzas at Longtino's at Sixty-Sixth and Nicollet in Richfield. He was working his way through law school. Tom Collins and his girlfriend came in after the fight. I had not told my family I would be fighting because I was to be ordained a Catholic priest one month later.

"I thought you won your last fight, Tommy," my brother said. "You look like you got turned every which way but loose."

"This fight was tonight," Tommy said. "And it was your brother!"

In the following weeks, Tommy asked me to show him a few tricks. He said I had the fastest hands he ever saw. I was now ordained, so he asked me to come to his fights for the golden gloves and give him my blessing. I did, and he won every fight and became the Upper Midwest Golden Glove light heavyweight champion. The nationals were in Kansas City that year, and I couldn't go down there. He lost his first fight, and I always thought that my priestly blessing gave him some psychological advantage. He thought he couldn't lose.

Back to grade school at Saint Peter's, we were having a great time. We had two outstanding nuns teaching us: Sister Georgetta and the principal Sister Mary Patrice. They were sisters from the Saint Joseph's Order. I would use the basics they taught me all the way through high school, college, grad school, even to my PhD.

One time in school, the paper chute, we thought, was packed up to the second floor. Our classroom was also on the second floor. I got the bright idea to climb into the chute and stomp down the paper. It turned out the chute was not packed all the way down, and when I jumped on it, it gave way, and the paper I was standing on broke away and went to the basement. I grabbed the opening on the second floor and hung on for dear life. Sister Mary Patrice was beside herself. I could not get out of the chute. The janitor, Henry Gessner, was called, and he tried to pull me out. The edge of the chute had a metal ridge, so when he pulled, I was being stopped by the ridge, and it was cutting into my legs. I finally decided that if I left one leg hanging down, I could avoid the ridge. Out I came. We were on our own for the rest of the afternoon because Sister Mary Patrice had such a headache she couldn't teach anymore that day.

Our basketball team was asked to play at halftime at the Minneapolis Lakers NBA. It was a real honor. I remember getting fouled and going to the line. In those days, I shot free throws underhand like George Mikan. When I made the free throws, the crowd went wild. I thought this was great. We got to sit under the basket for the rest of the Lakers game. As George Mikan was going around to make one of his famous hook shots, somebody put an elbow into him and bounced him across the court. George said, "Jesus Christ." Here we were, little Catholic grade school kids scandalized because George Mikan, our hero, swore. Later, as a priest in Hopkins, George Mikan was in my second parish as a parishioner. After Mass one day, he shook my hand, and I looked like a grade school kid again next to him.

At Saint Peter's, we had a Boy Scout troop led by Ray Monahan. We met at the school. One summer, we went to Many Point Scout Camp in Northern Minnesota. It would prepare me for when I worked two college summers at the Elk's Youth Camp on Big Pelican Lake in Brainerd, Minnesota. On one of the hikes, we came across an empty cabin, and some of the kids started breaking windows. I stood there and did nothing. There was no adult with our group, and I now know how quick vandalism can take place. Our scout troop was never invited back. They took up a collection, and we each had to pay for the vandalism. It prepared me for future restitution cases as a probation officer.

One year, we had a fund-raiser selling Mulligan stew tickets. The scout who sold the most tickets would get a nice green warm-up jacket. I wanted that jacket. I went door to door all through our neighborhood. I sold to all our friends and relatives. My aunt Neda Christian told me to be early and sell more tickets in the parking lot the evening of the Mulligan stew. I did and was the winner of the green warm-up jacket. My dad told me that with my sales skills, I would never starve.

A few days after winning the green warm-up jacket, we were playing "pump, pump, pull away" at school, and I was one of the last kids to be caught. Being fast, I could outrun most kids and sig and sag around them. I got a little too cocky and came too close to one of my pursuers. He grabbed my sleeve, and—*rip*—it came right off. The tear was so ragged that it could not be repaired. There went my beautiful green warm-up jacket. Another lesson learned in life.

When I was ten years old and in the fifth grade, we sold the farm. Our father was brought up during the Depression, so he only bought things he could pay for upfront. He paid for his used police cars with cash. He sold the 160 acres for 40,000 dollars. Today we can't buy one lot there for that much. He bought a house in West Richfield for twenty thousand and paid for it with cash. No bank was going to take it away from him. He bought 160 acres in Rosemont, a farming community south and east of the twin cities. He would sharecrop that land with a local farmer and receive one-third of the crop. He often said he got "one turd" of the crop. He bought the new farm for 35 dollars an acre, and we sold it years later for a nice profit.

Home

2201 West Sixty-Ninth Street
Richfield, Minnesota

It was 1947, and we moved to the west side of Richfield. Being a police officer, our dad had to live in the village he served. Across the street from us was the George and Christine Brening family. On the farm, George would always ask me how my gooseberry bushes were doing when he picked my dad up for a shift on the squad car. He always got a good laugh when I told him they were doing fine. I grow gooseberry bushes to this day up in our home in Avon, Minnesota.

One day, George gave me a pinch of snuff. He had always offered me one of those when he came to pick up our dad. He would get a good laugh out of his offering. This day, I took him up on it, and our dad nodded okay. I put the snuff under my lip. I still remember getting dizzy and falling into the box of overshoes in the hallway leading outside. I would not chew tobacco again until I was in college and working as a counselor at the Elks Youth Camp in Big Pelican Lake in Brainerd, Minnesota. I stopped that too when I was brushing my teeth one night and the stain from the chew would not come off my teeth. It did eventually.

George Brening was the police officer whom our dad told to shoot our dog Puppy when they thought he was attacking our pigs when the dog was actually protecting them. We held no resentment toward George. In fact, his son, Jim, and daughter, Dorothy, became our childhood friends. Jim was one of the people who helped me not start smoking. We used to work on his car, and he would have a cigarette hanging from his mouth with the smoke trailing up into his eyes. I thought that was a crazy habit. Because I thought I was an athlete, I didn't want my lungs to be damaged. I had no idea at that time about anything like cancer. Jim and Dick "Zeke" Justin would be the altar servers at my first Mass at Saint Peter's. Jim, unfortunately, would die of lung cancer in 2008. Zeke would have a heart attack and die watching the Minnesota Twins win the World Series in 1987. He had bet on the Twins to win it all in Las Vegas before the season, but his partner's wife had lost the ticket.

My brother Ken, as I said, was in the first graduating class from Saint Peter's Grade School. There was no high school at that time in Richfield. Most of the farm kids in the earlier days never went past the eighth grade. My dad was one of them. He often would come home and have our mother, who went to ninth grade, help him write up his police reports.

Many of Ken's graduating class would go to Washburn High School in Minneapolis. Some of the boys would go to DeLaSalle Catholic High School in downtown Minneapolis. Many of the girls could go to Holy Angels High School, which was all-girls at that time and right next to Saint Peter's Grade School. But Ken decided he wanted to become a Catholic priest just like our pastor Father Brand. He was off to Nazareth Hall, the minor seminary at 3003 North Snelling Avenue in Saint Paul. It was a boarding school, and we could see him once a month on visiting Sunday. He would come home for holidays and three months in the summer.

His terminology from an all-boys boarding school was different. Now everyone was called a "simp," short for *simpleton*. He had intramural sports, so they didn't play other schools but had teams put together for every sport, and every kid played. They had "A," "B," and "C" levels, so you played with kids of your own ability for the most part. It seemed kind of neat. It wasn't like varsity sports for a few of the top talented students as in most high schools. Ken was an excellent hockey player. He played against an all-priest team in high school but would go on to play for Michigan State University his freshman year of college, but he would then stop because he got married. We had a number of relatives who played hockey. I always claimed that Bill, Roger, and Dave Christian of Warroad, Minnesota, and Olympic fame were distant relatives. We always bought their hockey sticks and showed them off.

Two years after Ken went to the seminary, I would have to choose a high school. Father Brand and his assistant Father Vince Colon were great guys. Sister Georgetta and Sister Mary Patrice appeared to love their religious life. I too could help save the world.

In eighth grade, I was only five foot one, so most of the girls towered over me. We had eighth-grade parties, but I was usually not invited. I was not in the "in" group. I was into sports and was probably an average student. Father Brand said God was not going to knock me off my horse like he did Saint Paul on the road to Damascus. If I thought I wanted to be a priest, I should try it for a year and see if I liked it. I was free to do as I wanted.

Father Vince Colon coached our basketball team to the city finals, and he could kick a football a country mile. Hey, why not try the seminary and join Brother Ken?

Our parents were good Catholics. Our mother had converted from being a Protestant to a Catholic when she married our father. She had a German and Irish background. Our father was a traditional German, and we went to Mass every Sunday and holy days. The church had been the center of our life.

Every summer at the church picnic, we would load up our horses and give pony rides to the kids to help make money for the parish. The first time we did this, my father had to work on the squad car; so earlier, he loaded up the horses and brought us to the picnic grounds down by the Minnesota River bottoms. We set up a horse ring to lead the small kids around in a circle. Our father left us on our own. Ken was ten, and I was eight. Our father said they had a chicken dinner, and we would be called one by one to come up and eat the free dinner. After his eight-to-four shift, he would come back, and we would load up the horses before it got dark. As we were putting the horses in the trailer, he asked us if we went up to get our free chicken dinner. When we told him they never called us, he said, "Well, you will get a high seat in heaven for all your work."

The next year, we were at the picnic grounds again, and our father said, "Now, remember, they will call you around noon, and you go up and get your chicken dinner. And if they don't remember to call you, here is some money to buy a hot dog. And remember, if they don't call, you will get a high seat in heaven."

"Uh-ah", I said, "I got one of those last year!"

When I was in sixth grade, I made the varsity basketball team. I usually played when the game was either already won, or we were losing badly. One time, I was in for the last few minutes. Being five foot one, I was known for my speed, and I played in an under twelve league and scored a lot of points. I was one year too old, but they said, "You're small. Play there and get more experience." When I turned fifteen, I got a driver's license and got stopped for speeding out in Anoka, Minnesota, and had to go before the town judge that night. He said, "Didn't you play years ago in the under twelve league and score all those points against my team?" I said I did. He let me off with a warning. I was happy he didn't know I was too old for that league. He might have thrown the book at me. The arresting police officer was not too happy, though.

But back to sixth grade playing varsity. I knew I was with the big boys, so I had to move fast. I jumped out to steal a pass and got called for a foul. The referee came up to me and turned me around to see my number. He then laughed and put his fingers in my face and said, "The foul is on number 14."

One hand had four fingers up, and the other hand had one finger sticking out. His face was also down in front of mine, laughing along with the crowd. My boxing instincts took over, and I punched him right in the nose. Obviously, I was kicked out of the game and sent to the locker room.

I was already dressed when Father Brand came in and wanted me in the team picture. My picture with the team would hang in the school hallway. I was the only one in street clothes with a scowl on my face.

Father Brand would relay that temper incident to the rector of the seminary, Father Louis McCarthy; and for four years, each time I would go into the rector's office for my report card, he would ask me how my temper was coming along. I had no temper instances to report.

We had an eighth-grade graduation party, and I was chosen to do a comedy routine with Bud Sydness. Bud had been born with an open palate on the roof of his mouth. He said if he had kept his mouth shut as an infant, he would have been all right. It would have grown shut. The roof would have healed on its own. Instead, they operated, and he had a speech impediment that made him difficult to understand. He would tell a joke at the party, and I would repeat it. We were like Laurel and Hardy and went over big. Father Brand complemented us and asked us to say a few more jokes. Some of the girls were not too happy because we stole the show and mispronounced some of their words from the script. They sounded better our way.

In the fall of 1951, I would enter the minor seminary at the age of thirteen. In some ways, this was a mistake. I had a great family life going. Looking back, I should have gone four years to DeLaSalle Catholic High School like my brothers Dave and Mike and have a maturing social life with four more years of normal college life at Saint John's University. There would be advantages and disadvantages to both paths. In the long run, I think all turned out pretty well. I received a very good high school education and had plenty of time to read all the classics and play every sport. I have often said if I could do it all over again, I would not enter the seminary until after college. Missing out on interaction with girls is a problem for most priests even to this day.

In 2014, we had a Christian family reunion at Christian Park, which had been donated years ago by our grandmother and grandfather Therese and Frank Christian. One hundred and thirty-two people came from eight states. Brother Ed gave a history of the Christian family, and Father Ray Monsour celebrated the Mass. We had a pig roast in honor of the pig farm our family used to run.

Earlier, brother Ed had gone by the park and did not see a sign saying, "This is Christian Park." He went into the village hall and asked what the name of the park on the east side of Richfield was. They said they thought it was just East Park. Ed, as an attorney, reminded them that our grandparents had given the land to the village with the condition that it be named Christian Park or revert back to the Christian family.

Days later, he drove by, and a big sign said, "Christian Park." We had a good family, and I, as I now know, was too young to leave it for the seminary. But I did, and so the story of my life goes on.

Chapter 2

The Minor Seminary

Nazareth Hall, 3003 North Snelling Avenue
Saint Paul, Minnesota

The Lake Johanna dream began in1866 when Bishop Thomas L. Grace purchased the first forty-two acres at nineteen dollars per acre with the intention of building a seminary to prepare young men to become priests to minister "in this rugged land." It would take fifty-seven years for his goal to be realized.

In 1915, Archbishop John Ireland added forty-seven more acres at seventy-five dollars an acre. Archbishop Austin Dowling, with approval from the pope in Rome, began construction of the minor seminary in 1921 "out in the country" of Rose Township, which is now Roseville, a northern suburb of St. Paul.

The architects were Charles Maginnis and Timothy Walsh from Boston. They were the leading church builders of their day. They built the largest basilica in the country in Washington, DC, and many of the buildings on the University of Notre Dame campus.

The architects would call the project Job #518, Lake Johanna, Minnesota. The four-story structure would have accommodations for 250 people, including faculty, 12 nuns, approximately 200 students from ages 13 to 21, with a few older delayed vocations thrown in.

Raphael Guastavino was the ceiling maker with a herringbone pattern in the acoustical clay-tiled ceiling. He used secret formulas for the techniques and patented materials that fireproofed as well as beautified the vaulted ceilings in the foyer and chapel. Delicate patterns in the chapel ceiling incorporate images of flowers, crosses, and the Chi-Rho (Christ) symbols from early Christian days.

Archbishop Dowling also hired the Charles J. Connick's stained glass company in 1921 to create a series of windows. He wrote to Connick, saying he chose him because "the beauty of the chapel requires the finest glass windows."

There are eighteen windows in the Annunciation Chapel, twenty-four in the basement crypt area, and nine in the nuns' chapel. There were also six windows with angels and one rose window in the island chapel.

Nazareth Hall was built in the Northern Italian style described as Lombard Romanesque. It is a quiet style laid out in patterned red bricks, six hundred thousand in all.

The tower is the main focus and is visible above the treetops from across Lake Johanna. The 120,752-square-foot complex was completed, debt-free, and dedicated for classes on September 12, 1923. (Information from the Charles J. Connick Archives, Boston Public Library, and Dr. Mark Baden, professor, Northwestern College, formally Nazareth Hall).

In September, the Tuesday after Labor Day 1951, brother Ken and I were traveling from Richfield to the entrance of Nazareth Hall. Ken would be a junior in high school, and I was a freshman.

Tommy O'Rilley, a classmate from Saint Peter's Grade School, was supposed to come also, but he decided at the last minute against it. He was one of my thirty-one boxing matches. I beat him pretty badly and even hit him on top of the head to kind of show off. He was in tears when it was over. I felt bad about hitting him on top of the head. It was not the sportsmanship thing to do. I remember his father, who was a great guy, congratulating me on my victory. But I could see in his eyes that he didn't think the top-of-the-head hit was necessary.

Our cousin Gary, however, was joining me. I think my uncle Clarence, his dad, was behind his decision. Our father always said when people asked him about us going to the seminary, "They are getting a good education." I think it was his way of saying to his friends, *Don't get too excited about my sons studying to be priests.*

Anyway, with my brother Ken being an experienced hand and my old football blocking-guard cousin Gary, and my boxing background, I wasn't worried about being harassed, bullied, or picked on as a freshman.

I found out in a hurry that I was accepted. They gave me a nickname, "Little Windy." Apparently, brother Ken and another classmate, John, had a gas-passing contest in the main study hall when the supervising priest was walking away down the hall to say his mandatory daily prayers. Ken was called "Windy" for the rest of his stay at Nazareth Hall. Thus, I became "Little Windy."

We were housed in a large dormitory on the third floor. Joe Sweeney and Andy Otto were seniors and assigned to be our prefects. They were great guys. Our dean was Father Richard Moudry, another one of the good guys. Before we went to bed about 9:30 p.m., Father Moudry would give us a little pep talk.

We had to get up each morning at 6:00 a.m. When the wake-up bell sounded, we learned fast that you had to race to the community washroom if you didn't want to have to wait for a sink to wash, brush your teeth, shave, if you had whiskers (I started shaving in eighth grade). We had half an hour to do our morning duties because we had to be down in the beautiful chapel for meditation. We had to make our bed right away. We were taught to make a square corner on our sheets. I still make our bed that way. If your bed was sloppy, you would come back after breakfast and find it torn up and in a pile to be made over again, and it better be good this time. They used to say you had to be able to bounce a fifty-cent piece off the bed. It had to be that tightly made.

We had to make sure our area was clean and all our clothes picked up. There were twenty beds to a row. There were two rows. Your head was at the foot of the bed behind you. They didn't want you to be whispering to the person behind you, much less develop a "particular friendship." Then there was an aisle and another set of two rows with twenty beds. We each had a small dresser next to our bed and a small closet against wall. There were community mops, so you could dust your area and under your bed.

At six-thirty, we had meditation for a half an hour. Then at seven, we had daily Mass.

Meditation didn't work really well for most of us. We were so sleepy that it didn't take long, and many of the kids put their heads down on the front pew and fell back to sleep. It was tough to sit down because there was someone kneeling right behind you. The holy ones in our class always stayed awake and made us feel guilty, but not too guilty.

Mass was said by one of the faculty priests, but mostly by the rector, "Big Lou" McCarthy. He was six foot three and an overpowering figure. He was bald as an eagle and had piercing eyes. He also had a ready smile and a hearty laugh. In those days, they did not give a sermon or homily at the early mass, so we were out and ready for breakfast in a half an hour.

We had one of our classmates who held his thumbs and fingers together during the consecration of the Mass. We called him Saint John. He left before the major seminary, but I met him later in life at his sister's funeral, and he told me he taught out east at a Catholic high school. When I asked him what he taught, he said religion. I should have known. I just read his obituary, and it said he had become a deacon and taught religion in two different Catholic schools. His picture in his obituary showed him with the deacon's collar on. I guess it was as close to being a priest that he could get and be married.

After Mass was breakfast. The food was not too bad. The German nuns were working hard in the kitchen. Part of the student body took turns working as waiters. There was a list, and you had to look for your name each week to see if you were serving tables. Serving at tables assured you of more food after all the students were finished. A select few got to serve at the priests' table. This meant you got priests' leftovers, which were considerably better than student food. The faculty table was up on a raised platform. I think it was so they could look down on us and see if we were goofing off. It left us with the impression that we were second-class citizens, peons, and there was a distinct distance between us and them.

One time, we had grapefruit for breakfast. It was a rare treat. I was waiting on a table, so I got to eat later with extra grapefruit. Tom, one of my classmates, and I sat down and began to eat the extra grapefruit. Sure enough, we got into a contest. When I got to thirteen grapefruit halves, Tom was still on ten, when one of the German nuns came up to us and said, "Boys! That is no longer eating. It is gluttony!" Tom and I looked at each other and stopped eating. She who must be obeyed had spoken. Tom left after his junior year, and at six foot five, he went on to play basketball at DeLaSalle High School and Notre Dame University. I played golf with him after he left that summer, and he told me he hoped I rot in the seminary. I laughed then, but now I know what he meant. I heard he was very successful in business but got terminal cancer, and I heard he went around the world with his brother and then committed suicide. The word was, he jumped off his tall office building.

In the seminary, there was also another list we would have to check to see if we were on detail to clean up the grounds or clear an area for intramural sports like football. It was called work crew, and we were on it once a month. It was run by an older student and usually in conjunction with the paid janitor.

Monday through Friday, we had classes from nine to twelve. Lunch was at noon, and then classes would continue until three o'clock.

After three o'clock, there was free time except when you were scheduled to play intramural sports. Some kids went out bird-watching; others went for walks, played the piano, ping-pong, read, shot pool, or got in a card game (no legal poker allowed, which didn't stop some of us—my brother Ed lost big time when he bet the pot on an in-between, and he had an ace and a duce; he drew another ace and busted).

At four-thirty, the bell in the tower rang, and we all came in to shower, hopefully, and get ready for a study hall at five. Supper was at six. We all had to wear a shirt and tie for dinner. You can imagine what shape those ties were in after a few spills of gravy and sauces.

Dinner was fairly substantial. I always ate my dessert first. Usually, I was that hungry, but I learned quickly that there would be extra desserts around when people didn't eat theirs or didn't like them. I was assured of getting at least one extra dessert.

When the student waiter came with the family-style bowls, it was customary to dump them on one of our plates and send the server back for seconds. Sometimes it worked, and sometimes it didn't.

Behind the faculty table on the riser was the kitchen. Selected students waited on the priests and would receive any extras like steak or a nice cut of roast beef.

Supper started with a student reading another Latin scripture passage. Most of us couldn't understand the whole reading, but we often got the gist of it. The martyrology was read by one of the students at noon. These were stories on the saints who were killed for their faith. Listening to the readings, we often felt like martyrs ourselves. When it was over, we all said, "Deo gratias" ("Thanks be to God, it is over") and dug in to eat hardy. If you asked most of the student body what the reading was about, no one could really tell you for sure, mainly because they were not listening.

After supper, we were free to hang out until seven-thirty when the sacred study hall began. When we were freshman, there was a basketball league, and we sweated for an hour and then ran up to take a freshman shower, which consisted of a washcloth over your face and under your armpits. It was called a freshman shower because many of the newcomers didn't have good hygiene habits yet, and that was the extent of their bathing until Saturday.

At nine o'clock, we were on our way to bed. There was no talking after nine. It was called the grand silence. If you broke that rule, you were in big trouble. We were like inmates in prison or a mental asylum. It did serve as a control mechanism. We just washed up, brushed our teeth, did our daily duty, and hit the rack. Later, we called it doing hard time.

One time, I was out of bed tipping over a friend's bed. Our dean Father Moudry came out as I was heading back to my bed. He was ready to call the Riot Act on me, and I told him I had diarrhea, so he changed his tune and told me to go out to the bathroom as often as I needed to. It was a small lie which I would have to confess as a venial sin. It gave me something to confess that week during private confession.

The intramural sports teams were one of the better items of the day. They had teams divided up by talent. The good players were in the "A" league. Next was "B," and finally the "C" players. In the fall, as a freshman at 5 feet 1 and 110 pounds, I was put on a C league touch football team. Having played tackle peewee and midget football in grade school as an all-star in Richfield and Minneapolis leagues, I scored every time I got the ball. I soon was transferred to B and then A. We played only touch football, but in many ways, it was as rough as tackle.

We had intramural teams in just about every sport. We played football in the fall season, basketball and hockey in the winter, and softball fast pitch in the spring. Soccer was not popular, and it was not played in most of the schools. Baseball and handball, we played on our own. We had some pretty good pitchers. Intramural sports were a lot of fun because everybody could play, and you learned how to compete in a variety of sports. We did not have any varsity teams as such. In basketball, we had some teams come in from the outside and play a group of our best players. We also had teams by the year. For example, our freshman class had a lot of talent. One of our players was Tom, who I mentioned went on to play forward (six feet five) for Notre Dame University. Another star was Jerry. He was six feet as a freshman and could jump like a kangaroo. Jerry would later become High School Teacher of the Year in Apple Valley, Minnesota. He would follow me to college at Saint John's University. A story about Jerry and I will come later when we get to Saint John's.

Our high school freshman basketball coach was a college student by the name of Ken. He had been a high school star in Faribault, Minnesota. I was on the team as a guard, so all I had to do was bring the ball down and pass it to the big guys.

I grew six inches by my sophomore year and stood 5 feet 7 and weighed a 150 pounds. My full height in college eventually was five feet nine, and I weighed a 170 pounds.

In intramural teams, captains would be chosen by the athletic director Father Lenny. He was a strong farmer from Southern Minnesota, and he would play with one of the teams. We would bounce off him, and he would bang us right back. The captains would then get together and pick their team members. For the most part, the teams would be fairly even. You were assigned to an overall team and stayed with that designation throughout high school. The major teams were the Trojans, the Spartans, the Olympians, and the Marathons. At the end of the season, the major team with the most points would be the school champions. The sports helped us blow off steam and kept us healthy.

We played football up in what we called the big field. It was open by the woods and was full of sandburs. We played there anyway. One day, a car drove up by the big field. It had a middle-aged woman and two men in it. The two guys took turns getting in the back seat, and it looked like they were having fun with the woman, who also was enjoying the action. They thought they were in the woods, but it was our football field. It didn't seem to bother them that, within one hundred yards, there were thirty seminarians looking on. That night, we had something interesting to talk about for a change.

Freshman classes were Latin, religion, history, English, algebra, French or German, and Gregorian chant. Classes were tough, depending on the teacher. Some of the faculty were good, and some were not. We had so many subjects that we did not have much time to slack off.

Latin was number one, and our teacher was Father William. He was a real sportsman and knew Johnny Kundla, the coach of the Minneapolis Lakers, the National Basketball Association team. He had been in a major car accident, so he walked hunched over. And with his black cassock, he looked like a duck, so that was his nickname: "the Duck." The Duck had a test at the end of a marking period reading one hundred Latin words that we had to write the equivalent English word. If you got them all right, you would receive an A. We all studied hard, but we thought we needed a little extra help, so we had a system to cheat a little. At the end of the Duck reading the words, we would ask him to repeat the ones we had trouble with. After he read the word, the person who knew the word would whisper it to the one ahead of him, and we would write down the answer. Here we were, studying to be priests and cheating to get a better grade. It never worked. No one ever got all the words, but we had another venial sin to confess that week.

I had a lazy eye and was asked by my eye doctor to wear a patch over my good eye to strengthen the bad eye. It was hereditary. My brother Dave had one also. In looking at old pictures, I saw Great-Uncle Charlie Christian had one too. Dave had his weak eye operated on, but it didn't do any good. The doctor then wanted to operate on his good eye to weaken it, so the two eyes worked together. My parents didn't think that was a good idea, so Dave and I had our lazy eyes all our lives.

I would wear the patch when I was in church in the morning. No one really saw me except the people around me. My lazy eye would get better, but as soon as I stopped wearing the patch, the eye would go right back to following the good eye. That put a strain on the good eye, and I eventually had to have glasses to help the good eye. The Duck found out I should be wearing a patch over my good eye, so he made me wear it in his Latin class. I would get a headache if I wore it too long. When we would have one of his quickie tests, I always pulled the patch up so I could see to write the answers. He never caught on, but he took a liking to me, and it helped when the grades came out.

We had people in our freshman class from all over the Midwest. Some of the bishops from neighboring dioceses wanted their seminarians trained at Nazareth Hall. Many of them had gone there themselves.

Being thirteen years old and away from home made a number of kids homesick. Each day, we would learn that another student had left and gone home. Some wet their bed, and others cried themselves to sleep. I had my brother and cousin there, and I told myself that I was getting a good education and playing all the sports I loved. So when a homesick feeling came over me, I sucked it up and carried on. Besides, I had a whole load of new friends who made the time pass quickly.

On the first, third, and fifth Sundays of the month, we could have visitors. My parents came along with my three brothers or an aunt. One time, our aunt Jo brought chicken. It was good. Later, we found out it was rabbit. It had four legs. Visitors brought food packages that we could share or hoard until the next visiting Sunday. It was always harder that Sunday night because you knew you had to stay, and your visitors went home.

Kids had their sisters come to visit, so we were all eyes checking out the beautiful girls.

Our social life was very limited. On Saturday nights, we would have a movie. It was an old Randolph Scott flick. Father Karl was the organizer for this event. He taught German, and his nickname was "the Bear." He was a burly guy, and he and I would shake hands, and he would try to crush my hand. I usually had a standoff with him. I would never let him think he had the upper grip (or hand).

One day, I came into the dormitory, and Tom had a funny-acting student named Leon hanging out the three-story window by the ankles. Leon was one of our characters in our class and had a high squeaky voice. He was screaming and wiggling, and I told Tom that he might shake himself loose and fall three stories. Tom laughed and brought Leon inside.

We started with fifty-two freshmen, but the ranks soon thinned out. Yes, we were too young to be away from home. The minor seminaries are now a thing of the past. We really did not know or were mature enough to know if we really wanted to be a priest. We thought it might be a good idea at the time.

Toward the end of our freshman year, one of my classmates and I hit it off, and we hung around together. In fact, during our summer vacation, I went over to his house in Osseo, Minnesota, for a sleepover. His name was Harold. He was on a C league basketball team and had a hook shot that served him well. The high school newspaper called the *Puer Nazarenus* ("The Boy of Nazareth") wrote up some of the sporting events. It happened to cover Harold's game. The reporter honed in on Harold's accomplishments and said Harold, "the Hooker," was deadly with his hook shot. As you could guess, Harold became known as "Harry the Hooker" from then on. It now has another meaning, so it doesn't work for him anymore.

The spiritual director for Nazareth Hall was Father Ambrose. He was known by the student body as "Amby." He had a bad habit of saying, "All right, all right." We all imitated him by pulling our right ear like he did and saying, "All right, all right" all the time.

At the end of our first year, Father Amby called me in to his office and said I had to stop hanging out with Harry the Hooker. He said I had to be friends with my whole class and not one particular student. I told him that I thought I was friends with all my classmates, but Harold and I liked to write short stories for the *Puer Nazarenus*, our student paper, and we did enjoy talking and hanging out, but that I would try to spread my friendship around more. Little did I know what a particular friendship could also involve. He spoke in general about particular friendships in one of his spiritual conferences, but we all thought it was just a suggestion to not be exclusive with your time. We did not even know that homosexuality could be applied to a relationship. I would find out about that at a later date.

Harry the Hooker came back for his sophomore year but left before Thanksgiving. He went into the military and served in Korea. Harold had me serve as godfather to his first son, Allen. Jerry, another good friend, had me serve as godfather to his first son, Timothy, also.

In the seminary, we were told not to be godfather to anyone's children because we could not be available if we had to take over rearing a child Catholic. Being the doubting Thomas, I refused to follow that suggestion. But as it turned out, I did not have to step in at any time. Given my time, moving around the country and all, I kept in touch as godfather with our Easter letter, and that was about all. Their parents did an excellent job of rearing them, so I was never called upon to step in and make sure they were living up to good Christian standards.

As I stated, our freshman class had fifty-two students. By the time we were ordained, there would only be six.

I can't say too many times that going in the seminary at the age of thirteen was definitely not a good decision. We were way too young. Those of us who made it were not mature enough to do our best work. We had little experience with girls because we were told not to date. Half the population we would be working with would be women. Wives, mothers, single women, nuns, teenage and elementary-age girls would make up many of the people we needed to serve. Emotionally and psychologically, we were also immature. It may be one of the reasons that some priests have had problems with abnormal sexual behavior. I will address this idea more in-depth later in this book.

As I said, one good thing was we had plenty of time to read and study. As my father had said, we got a good education. He had only an eighth-grade education. He always said get a good education. No one can take that away from you. He had gone through the Great Depression, and it affected his approach to life. When he bought something, he always paid cash. It even happened when he sold the farm in 1947 and bought and paid in full for our home at 2201 West Sixty-Ninth Street in West Richfield.

Another positive feature in the seminary was the friendships we were able to form over the years. A number of friends are still in touch after all these years.

We also became fairly efficient in a number of sports. Spending high school in intramural sports let us play every sport we wanted to. Later in college at St. John's University, I would find out how not playing varsity sports would affect me.

I completed my freshman year, and we were sent home for the summer months. This was a welcome break from the seminary routine. We first met with our home pastor Father William Brand. He welcomed us back to Richfield. He may have expected us to attend daily Mass, but we got jobs and did not see him except for Sundays until the end of the summer.

I worked for a local nursery, cutting sod, loading it on trucks, and hauling it to people with new homes needing lawns. I also laid the sod when they were behind. I could keep a straight line and had a little touch for how it should be laid to look good. I gave all my money each paycheck to my mother. She had been a bookkeeper for Munsingware Shirt Factory in Minneapolis, and she gave us interest and any spending money we ever needed. She also did our taxes until we were adults.

Summer was over too soon, and we reported back to our pastor Father Brand. He had to write a report on how we behaved during the summer. He laughed and said he hardly saw us but always put out a good report on me.

Sophomore year was the year of the "wise fools." We thought we knew everything. We were told right away that we were going to be watched very closely, and we could not get away with anything. Although we lost a number of classmates who decided to not come back to the seminary, we also gained students who left their other high school to come to the seminary. Three were Bob Burke, Pat McManus, and Charlie Froehle. Bob was smart and could play hockey, and Charlie also was smart and was a good softball pitcher. I was his catcher, and we won most of our games with our battery. Pat McManus came from Duluth, Minnesota, and wore a black leather jacket and walked down the hallways with two of his Duluth gang members, intimidating all in his path. He also was very intelligent and was later sent to Rome to study theology. He became bishop material. He eventually would resign from the priesthood, marry, and become the Commissioner of Corrections for the State of Kansas.

The freshman class brought in new blood. One of the people I remembered from the past year's visiting Sunday. He watched intently as I played pool with my chartreuse tie on with a big red rose in the middle. His older brother Mike was already in the seminary. A friend for life, Rufus Ambrose North, had fiery red hair and a wit unmatched in our day. We called him Ruf or the Red Man. He would play a significant role in my future.

My brother Ken was now a senior, and I could see he was growing a little tired of the seminary routine. During the summer, he hung out with his Richfield and Bloomington friends: Jim Brening, Zeke Justin, and John Rezak, among others. They were into cars and spent a lot of time at car shows and stock car races.

One Sunday, soon after school started, Ken and a classmate decided to skip High Mass and instead shoot buckets in the school gym. They had been to the 6:30 a.m. Mass, and the priests were gone out to help at other parishes, except for the priest celebrating the High Mass. Little did they know that the dean of Discipline, Father Lenny, had stayed behind also and was hiding up in the balcony overlooking the pews below. He noticed that two spots next to each other were missing. He proceeded to search the building. It didn't take him long to hear the basketball pounding on the floor and against the hoop. They were snagged. They would be written up in his snag book and reported to the rector, Big Lou.

Monday at dinner, the angel of death was sent by the rector to Ken and John's tables. The angel of death was just a student waiting on the priests' table. He was told to tell Ken and John to see the rector right after supper. We had a joke that as soon as we saw the angel of death come down from the faculty table, I would grab the ketchup bottle and open it and pretend to put a little ketchup on a table leg. As in the days of Moses, the angel of death "passed over" the homes of the Israelites who had the blood of a lamb on their doorpost. This time, I couldn't get to my brother's table leg in time. The angel of death had struck.

Ken went into Big Lou's office in fear and trembling. Big Lou confronted him about skipping High Mass. He then made the mistake of asking Ken if he liked it here at Nazareth Hall. Ken didn't hesitate and said, "No!" He had had enough, and being a priest and going through the seminary routine was no longer in his cards.

Big Lou didn't hesitate either. "Then you better leave now!" Ken was gone that evening. Our father came to pick him up, and he was history. He went up to St. John's Prep School in Collegeville, Minnesota, to finish his senior year. He then went his freshman year to St. John's University. From there, he went into the army and served two years in Fort Leonard Wood, Missouri. After that, he went to Michigan State, played Division 1 hockey for them one year, got married, and graduated in criminal justice. He came back to Minnesota and became a Bloomington police officer.

Ken was happy to be out of what we called Nazareth "hole." It was now one Christian brother kicked out of the seminary. As you will see, it will not be the last. But I was now established with classmates and friends, and I could carry on. It was my job to hold the fort and one day be ordained and save the world. Ken's partner in crime, John, was able to convince Big Lou that he was truly repentant and had been to Mass at six-thirty and thought skipping High Mass was not a capital offense, so he was allowed to continue as long as he kept his nose clean. John made it through the minor and major seminaries and was ordained with the class of 1961. He later resigned as a priest for the Roman Catholic Church and became an Episcopal priest. Of course, he then could get married.

As a sophomore, we lived up to the title "wise fools." We would short-sheet classmates' beds and laugh when they tried to get into their bed at night. Short-sheeting took place when one took the second sheet and folded it over and put it on the blanket like all was okay. The person would try to get into bed but would be stopped halfway down.

We also would take oranges from the refectory and throw them from one end of the dormitory to the other. One time, Mike and I were playing catch, and Mike missed. The orange splattered on the far wall, and the next morning, Mike's brother Charlie, who was the student prefect, had Mike clean it up and promise not to play catch anymore. Charlie's other prefect was Roger Hessian. We called him Hoot after the movie actor Hoot Gibson. Roger was from Bell Plaine, a farming community. He had red hair and talked slow as if he had a piece of straw in his mouth. When we had our Saturday night Western movies with Randolph Scott and Hoot Gibson, it didn't take long for Roger to become "Hoot." Years later, in my first assignment as a priest, I would be second assistant to Hoot, who was first assistant at Saint Rose of Lima Parish in Roseville, Minnesota. Hoot and I have been friends ever since.

I made it through my sophomore year despite the dean of Discipline, Father Lenny. We called him Leaping Lenny because he would put himself on one of the intramural teams, and being an old farm boy, he would roughhouse with us on the football field and basketball court. One time in physical education, he had us in a circle and was throwing the basketball at us at full speed ahead. I would throw it right back at him. He told me that I was a wise guy and would say and do things off the top of my head. He said if he ever thought I was premeditating some of my behavior, I would be in for it. He finally got his wish my senior year.

We had one student, Stanley, who was small and physically thin and out of shape. We called him "Stan the Man." He was a scholar and had won the Sierra one-hundred-dollar prize for an essay on why he wanted to be a priest. The Sierra Club continues to promote religious vocations. Leaping Lenny took the basketball and fired it at Stan and just about knocked him over. He then took the ball and did it again. At the time, I almost stepped in and came to Stan's rescue, but then I thought Leaping Lenny was trying to make a point of getting Stan to get into the swing of things. It didn't work.

Stan the Man did save me one time. In the basement of the church was the crypt. It consisted of a number of small altars where the priests at the seminary could say their daily Mass. You know that they got a stipend each time they said Mass. We would serve for them. We got nothing. Our old pastor Father Brand used to give us fifty cents to serve Mass back in St. Peter's Parish when we were in grade school.

Stan the Man was the sacristan for the priests. One time, he caught me finishing off the wine left by the priest that I had served for that morning. If he reported me, I would get kicked out. I told him if he gave me some slack, I would never do it again. Stan came through for me. I owed him one.

Junior year was more of the same. If you wanted to be a priest, you had to put up with the boring life of a seminarian. Now, there were two years of students under us, so you could show them the way and play sports with more competition. One of the new freshmen was my brother Ed. He and I had grown up together on the farm and on the West side of Richfield. He was an excellent student and would receive all A's on his report card. His conduct took after me, however, and we both would get U's or "Unsatisfactory." Leaping Lenny figured Ed was a Christian brother and followed Ken and my style of behavior. Ed had a good class, and we had a lot of fun playing every sport. Ed was a good hitter in softball, a good shot in basketball, and an excellent passer in football. I was quicker than him, but I hit the singles and doubles, and he hit the long ball. After all the seminary days were over, Ed said he might have done it all over again based on the friends he made and the education he was able to receive. Ed went six years to Nazareth Hall, two years of college, along with the four years of high school. I would not be able to match him with the two years of college at the "hole," but I would outdo him in the major seminary.

Summers, we were free to go home and work. I worked at Ammot Well Drilling as a helper and a sodbuster, Raunhorst Construction as a laborer, Elk's Youth Camp as a waterfront director, and Waverly, Minnesota, as athletic director. They were good jobs, and we were able to save money and pretty well do what we wanted. Each year at the end of the summer, Father William Brand would continue to write up a report on how we behaved during the summer months. He knew we went to church on Sundays and worked all week, but he rarely saw us besides that. He would joke about that but always gave us a good report.

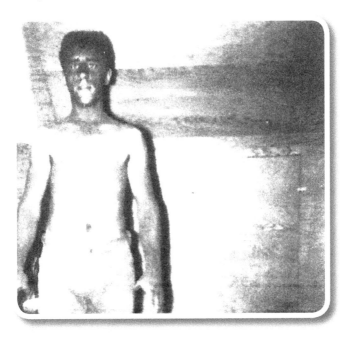

Tom working as a sod buster in the summer. He later
liked working as a well-driller's helper better.

Tom's friend Ray Monsour and Tom working as
waterfront and activities counselors at the Elk's youth
camp at Big Pelican Lake in Brainard, Minnesota.

I did not date, which was a no-no. I was immature, so girls were
to be looked at but not touched. But on occasion, some of the kids
we had gone to school with at Nazareth Hall and had quit would
invite us to parties, and as a group, we would do things that included
girls. Sitting next to them in a car with my arm around them came
as close as I would get until, one time, we were going to a party, and
friends of ours stopped and picked up two of their girlfriends. One
got in the back seat with me and started kissing me all the way to the
party. On the way home, she did the same thing. I just sat there and
enjoyed it.

However, two of my classmates from Nazareth Hall, Bob and
Pete, and I were cruising along in downtown Saint Paul one summer
evening, and there were two girls walking down the street. Bob was

driving, so I told him to stop and "let's at least talk to the girls." Before he could think about it, Bob stopped, and I jumped out of the car. Talking and laughing with the girls was a thrill. One had her billfold in her hand, and for some reason, I said, "Let's see what your name is." She pulled her billfold away and started to be upset. I said, "No problem. Let's be cool," and I told them it was nice talking to them. We drove off and had a good laugh.

A few days later, Bob called me at home and said a probation officer was at his house with a complaint from the two girls. They had taken down Bob's license plate and called the cops. I told Bob to put the investigator on the phone, and I would handle it. After all, my father was a Richfield police officer, and I had been stopped a number of times speeding in Richfield, and I was always able to come out okay. The officer would tell my dad, and he would chew me out and tell me not to do it again. I never got a ticket. So this time, I talked to the juvenile probation officer and told him Bob and Peter had nothing to do with it, and it was all my fault. I was still seventeen, and Bob and Pete were eighteen. As adults, they could be in deep trouble.

Over the phone, the probation officer said okay, but I would have to meet with him and appear in juvenile court in Ramsey County. If this got out to my family or Nazareth Hall, my seminary days were over. So I went to the juvenile probation department and met with the investigator. I explained to him that it was all my doing, and it was not too smart on my part. I also told him that I was in the seminary, and he, being a good Catholic, began to smile. He told me if I kept my nose clean until I turned eighteen, he would dismiss the harassment charge. I called Bob and Pete and told them the good news. We all went back to the seminary that September and told no one. Pete quit at the end of his senior year, but Bob went on to the college and postgraduate part of the seminary but decided at the last minute not to be ordained. I would meet yet another fate.

Nicknames

Because we were in the seminary 24-7 for nine months and had nothing better to do, we often came up with nicknames for professors and students. It made for good humor and made life more tolerable.

We would "cap" someone, and some of the names stuck to this day. I went from Little Windy to Chris to Tris to Hairy (arm and chest hair) to Harold (long for Hairy) to Blackie (the hair again and the tough-guy role I accepted because we had too many milk-toast types in the seminary). Many people call me that even today. One of my friends called our home years later, and my wife answered. He said, "Is this Blackie's wife?" She knew who they were talking about.

Nicknames for the priest professors included the Bear, big burly Father Karl, Black Tom (heavy, dark beard), Big Lou (six feet five), Pinky (looked like a rabbit), JDQ, Leaping Lenny, Curly, Father O (for zero), Socksy, Harpo, Bucky, Butch, Kufu, the Duck, and Amby.

Student nicknames were Windy (my brother Ken), Little Windy (me), Blossum or Bones (my brother Ed), the Black Man (me again), the Red Man, the Baby Hippo, Bunless, Iggy, Stan the Man, Itch, Big Daddy, Tim Mouthy, Antoine, Valentino, the Great Lover, Dog, Big Moe, Joseph, the Simple, the Arab (Lebanese nationality), Crazy Bob, Doc (who became a bishop), Peter the Wolf, Toby Prin (based on an old TV personality), Harry the Hooker, H (for "honest") Jake, Puddy, the Feeler (a person who walked around with his robe open all the time), Ziggy, and Tarzan. Living together in a seminary caused us to be creative when we saw someone do or act in a certain way. It helped to live with the boredom.

The Snag Book

Leaping Lenny had a book we called the snag book. In it, he wrote up all the bad behavior he saw as dean of Discipline. That is why my brother Ed and I always got an Unsatisfactory in conduct. One time, Ed dumped a classmate in the big garbage barrel in the study hall as the kid was trying to sharpen his pencil. You see,

Leaping Lenny, or whoever was in charge of study hall that evening, usually walked around saying their breviary prayers and often left the study hall and walked down the other hallways. When they did that, we could sneak up and open the dean's desk drawer and quickly read the snag book. One time, Iggy and I had a beard-growing contest to see who could go the longest before we were told to shave. Iggy won, and Leaping Lenny wrote me up for being "characteristic," trying to grow sideburns and look like a tough, cool guy. We could often tell what our report-card conduct was going to be by looking in the snag book. You could get rated "good," "average," or "unsatisfactory."

It was one of those times my senior year that I snuck a look at the snag book and saw I got a DIJ. That was not good. It meant I would be "dropped in June." Kicked out like brother Ken. Along with me were some of my compatriots in crime. Big Lou, the rector of the seminary, had gotten tuberculosis (TB) and was sent off to a sanitorium. Father James (Kufu) was made acting rector. That left it to Leaping Lenny, the dean of Discipline, to clean house. All the wise guys were gone. Knowing ahead of time, I was planning my strategy. Kufu was our history teacher, and he liked me ever since I wrote the Gettysburg Address out on an envelope like President Lincoln and gave the presentation in class. I used a high-pitched voice like I heard Lincoln had. I made a top hat. By the way, it was the same time I was in the beard-growing contest with Iggy, so I tried to look like President Lincoln to the best of my ability. Kufu loved it, and I got an A in history that quarter.

As I entered the rector's office for the final report card, I had to appear shocked when Kufu said the faculty had decided that I was expelled. Kufu said he liked me and was surprised, but the faculty had decided. I then went up to Amby, the spiritual director, and of course, he already knew my fate. He was no help. He said I came in as a freshman with an inferiority complex, but by the time I was a senior, I had a superiority complex. I had no comeback to that one. Guilty as charged. I was gone. History. Four years of hard time was over. I was a free man, but no place to go. It was June, and all the college freshman classes around the state were already filled.

It was time to check in with our local pastor Father William Brand. He gave me good advice: Go to St. John's University where my brother Ken had gone and see if they would give me special consideration based on the fact that I was just told I could not go back to Nazareth Hall. Go to regular college for four years, and if I still felt I was called to be a priest, then enter the major seminary. It made sense. I could now act like a normal college student, play varsity sports, date girls, have a beer, and live again.

Saint John's University

Collegeville, Minnesota

St. John's University was located ninety miles from our home in Richfield. Brother Ken had gone there for the rest of his senior year of high school after he was kicked out of Nazareth Hall. He stayed for his first year of college, and then he went into the army.

So why not me?

In 1846, Archabbot Boniface Wimmer, OSB, established the first Benedictine monastery in the United States: Saint Vincent Archabbey in Latrobe, Pennsylvania. He went on to build ten Benedictine communities throughout the United States. In 1856, he sent five monks to the Minnesota territory. They settled along the banks of the Mississippi in St. Cloud. St. John's University was founded in 1857 by these Benedictine monks, who actually traveled to Minnesota from Germany. Native tribes were induced to move north, and there was a large population of German immigrant farmers, and both needed to be served by the monks. They were encouraged to come over by Father Francis Pierz (1785–1880), one of the few priests in the area. A local town in Central Minnesota, Pierz, is now named after him. Bishop Joseph Cretin (1799–1857) from St. Paul also talked the German bishops into sending the monks along with money to start a school. One of the batches of money, rumor has it, was supposed to go to the Benedictine nuns in St. Joseph, Minnesota, to help them with a school for girls. The monks pocketed the money for their own needs; after all, in those days, I presume, they may have thought girls belonged at home, rearing children and working in the kitchen.

The money for the nuns came from the Ludwig Verlin Society in Germany. Archabbot Wimmer used it to buy the Indian Busch property overlooking Lake Sagatagan, which is now the major part of St. John's University and abbey. The first abbot of St. John's Abbot, Rupert Seidenbusch, OSB, was called the "Abbot of Indianbush" when Archabbot Boniface Wimmer gathered the new community together to begin St. John's Abbey.

Meanwhile, the German nuns had already left Germany in June of 1852. They arrived in the United States on July 3 and got to St. Joseph, Minnesota, on July 4. Due to the lack of funds, the nuns would not be able to start the girls' school until 1913. By 1915, a four-year college was in place. Sister Mariella Gable, OSB, writes in *In League with the Future: The First Fifty Years* (1964), "We shouldered a staggering debt. Paying interest on interest … Hardest to bear was the spectacle of the many needs for college expansion for which there was no money."

Today St. John's has about 1,200 students and is a liberal arts college. It is located in Collegeville ten miles from St. Cloud, one of the largest cities after Minneapolis and St. Paul. It is known for some of its famous alumni, like Senators Eugene McCarthy and David Durenberger, Representative Mark Kennedy, and President Obama's chief of staff Denis McDonough. St. John's football coach, John Gagliardi, won more games in the NCAA than anyone else (489). John Gagliardi retired at 86 in 2012.

Marcel Brewer from Switzerland was the architect for the university's famous church built in 1957. It has a beautiful banner bell tower, and the interior has no pillars and is made of poured cement. The front stained glass windows represent the full Catholic Church liturgical year.

Here, I came to St. John's University in June of 1955, thinking I could start regular college as a freshman. The dean of Admissions was a kindly monk named Father Gunther Rolfson. When I told him I would like to enroll for the September freshman's class, he gently told me the class had already been selected in March, and they were full. He asked where I went to high school and why I was so late in coming. I told him I was from Nazareth Hall in St. Paul, the minor seminary, and had been expelled. He brightened up and asked if I still wanted to be a priest. I said I did but was advised to go to a regular college first. He said they had room in Saint Anselm Hall, their minor seminary. He quickly told me their seminary was just like a regular college, and I would find it much different from Nazareth Hall. He smiled when he said that. I would take classes with the regular college and be able to participate in all the programs, including sports. I swallowed hard and thought I would give it a shot. Here I was, back in the seminary again.

Father Gunther enrolled me in Saint Anselm Hall and said, "We will see you in September." He proved to be right. I was able to play sports, participate in all the college activities, and with a fake ID, drink beer at the El Paso, a bar in St. Joseph, Minnesota. The dean was Father Otto Zimmerman, and his assistant was Father Francis Studer, two great guys. Father Otto was a quiet, scholarly monk with a quick smile and an easygoing personality. He taught Latin, and with all the Latin I had in high school, I was able to translate Cicero in places where he was stumped. Father Francis had graduated from West Point Military Academy, so he was a little more straight-laced, but he was also friendly and helpful.

I had to live in a dorm and study in a study hall, but I was basically free as a bird. The regular college students called St. Anselm Hall "anslime hall," but coming from Nazareth Hall—which, if you remember, we called Nazareth hole—I felt right at home. One short-coming was no dating girls. I saw plenty at events and talked to them and related to a couple of girls set up by friends, but it was like a onetime thing. Overall, I was busy and happy.

College boxing had been stopped the year I came because a student had been killed on the boxing team at the University of Wisconsin, so I went out for wrestling. I had no high school experience, and I had to rely only on my speed and strength. My farm days of lifting heavy things paid off. I learned a few holds, and as a backup, I was able to help the team win the Minnesota Intercollegiate Athletic

Conference (MIAC) championship the two years I was there. The student coach, Larry Betzler, a four-year state champion, said if I had stayed all four years at St. John's, I could have been a contender.

I also went out for football and track. In track, I thought I was fast and was able to beat everyone in the 100-yard dash until Cyril Paul came out with my encouragement. Cyril had been a teacher in Trinidad and a police officer in the Bahamas. He was seven years older than I was. In trials, I ran 10.8 hundred yards. As I was ahead of everyone, I saw Cyril pass me and beat me by 10 yards. He ran 9.8 hundred yards and went on to become the MIAC champion in the 100, 220, and anchored the 4-by-400.

I also went out for spring football. Football Coach John Gagliardi had seen me wrestle and asked me to come out for football, but as a freshman, I got no real notice. I told him I was out in the fall, but he said he would give me a real chance in spring practice. Our 191-pound wrestler had broken his ribs, and at 170 pounds, I was asked to wrestle in his place. I did okay until I met the reigning 191 champion from St. Thomas University, Dick Gurtek. He pinned me in the second period. He had come down in weight from 220 to 191 pounds. I would get on the scales with my winter coat on and still only weighed 175. It was the only time I would be pinned.

Now it was time for the finals to go to the state. I decided to stay at the 191 weight, although I only still weighted in at 170 dripping wet. I won the two preliminary in house matches but then had to face Roger Ludwig, who had healed his rib injury and was ready to come back. He did weigh 191 pounds; although, like Gurtek, for football, he weighed in at 220 pounds. He also would be all-MIAC tackle in football.

We used to lose weight in order to qualify at a lower class and then do better on the mat. I got down to 147 for one match. It was against Macalester College. I came out strong and picked up my opponent over my head. It was like the pros did it. It looked good, and the crowd liked it. But it was not a smart move in amateur wrestling, as I was about to find out. As I gently laid my opponent down for the pin, I was too far over him, and he turned me over with him, and he had me in a pin hold. As he clamped me tightly, I thought I was a goner. I arched my head and neck, but it looked like it was to no avail. In the stands, I heard one of my classmates from Nazareth Hall, Jerry "Tarzan" Eibner, shout for me to come on, get loose, and win the match. Jerry had left Nazareth after high school the same time I had been kicked out. I was glad to see him again as a freshman at St. John's. He would go on to become the Minnesota Teacher of the Year in Apple Valley High School. Now on the mat, I heard him and gave it one more time to get away. I arched and spun and reversed my position and won the match. I would always remember that experience, and when our kids later played sports, I always exhorted them to give their all because I knew it would inspire them to give it that last best effort.

The final match for the 191 position for the state meet now had Roger Ludwig as my final opponent. Roger was strong, but coming from a small high school and like me, he had limited experience at wrestling. I was faster, and he had trouble keeping track of me. It was a close match when he picked me up over his head like I had done in the other match, but I squirmed, and he dropped me. But then he fell on me by accident. The match was stopped to give me time to recover because of his illegal move. I wasn't the same and lost 9 to 7. It was then that the football coach John Gagliardi came over to me and said, "I want you out for football."

That spring of 1956, I was there. John wanted me to try out for linebacker. He saw how reckless I was in wrestling, and he wanted me to dart into the backfield and make some tackles for a loss. If I had stayed with his plan, I may have ended up with a concussion or two. But I told him I wanted to try out for halfback with my speed and all city and all suburban honors back in grade school.

Not having played high school tackle football left me at a disadvantage. Spring football in Minnesota means you play on a muddy field. True to his word, John gave me a shot at halfback. On the last play of scrimmage that day, I got the ball and raced through the line and avoided the linebacker. I ran down the sidelines with only the safety to beat. He happened to be a senior by the name of Al Jirele. He would become Vice President Walter Mondale's press secretary. He had the angle on me, so I had two choices: run into his shoulder and try to keep going, or duke him and avoid the tackle. Unfortunately, I chose the latter. I duked him, and he missed me. My knee, however, twisted because my cleats stuck in the mud, and I saw stars as my ligaments and cartilage tore. I would never play tackle football again. I went to the hospital the next day because I could not walk on it. They wrapped it and gave me a brace to wear. I did wrestle my sophomore year with my leg shaved and taped ligaments, but I was not very effective. The opposing team kept yelling, "Go for his leg." All taped up, my knee looked like a balloon. We wrestled St. Cloud State, and my opponent was a military veteran with tattoos on his arms. I thought, *What have I gotten myself into now?* I put my head down and used my speed and beat him. I learned looks can be deceiving.

I would go on with a brace and play softball in the summers for the Glass Stem, a Bloomington bar, until I ran into another out-fielder catching a ball between us. Bill Noleen was a good hitter but mediocre fielder, so I was told to catch everything I could get to. Sure enough, the batter hit a line drive right between us. I ran into Bill's territory and caught the ball just as he ran into me. I held on to the ball, but my leg went out of joint with the brace on. They had to carry me out to the back of a station wagon, and I bounced all the way to the hospital. The doctor opened my knee and removed all the torn ligaments and cartilage. He told me I would have to strengthen all the other muscles to compensate.

One good thing that came out of my injury was the fact that John Gagliardi decided that too many people were getting hurt in practice, and he would not let anyone tackle in practice. He became famous for his unorthodox style of coaching. He did not have a whistle, he didn't believe in a weight room, he never cut anyone, all suited up for home games, and every senior was a captain (he said it looked good on their résumés).

The best thing that happened to me at St. John's University is that I met Raymond George Paul Monsour. He was from a Lebanese family on the west side of St. Paul, Minnesota. The first weekend at St. John's, we could leave and go home. Nazareth Hall, as you remember, had one visiting Sunday a month, but we stayed on the grounds. Needing laundry and more clothes, I let the dean of Anselm Hall, Father Otto, know my intentions. No problem. I put a note on the bulletin board asking if anyone wanted to hitchhike to the Twin Cities.

Up came Ray.

We have been good friends, like brothers, since 1955. I spoke at his celebration of his fiftieth year as a priest. At our first meeting, I told Ray if we got a ride to Minneapolis, I had a car. (No freshman was allowed cars on campus, but I later brought my car up and hid it on a farm of a friend of ours and a fellow wrestler, Fran Bruggman). I would drive him over to St. Paul. He said if we got a ride to St. Paul, his brother Joe would drive me over to Richfield. Fortunately, we got a ride to St. Paul.

In those days, we could hitchhike everywhere and not have a worry that people would not pick us up. As we walked into Ray's house, his mother, Sadie, asked, "What's your name?"

When I said *Tom*, she said, "Your name is Tanose." If you remember Uncle Tanose on *The Danny Thomas Show*, you know *Tanose* is "Thomas" in Arabic. Sadie proceeded to feed us a number of types of meat, potatoes, bread, salads, and desserts. Then she asked if I had any brothers or sisters. When I said I had four brothers, she proceeded to pack a bag of food for them. Since then, my family has eaten more Lebanese food than you can believe. We often have what is called a La Ha Mishua. It is lamb, chicken, and beef on skewers with onions, peppers, and mushrooms. You eat that with Lebanese flat bread, garlic sauce, and sloutah (lettuce with garlic sauce). Jokingly, I told my future wife, Bernice, that I would marry her if she learned how to cook Lebanese food. She followed Sadie around and learned quickly. Sadie could not read or write, so she told Bernice, "You use this and that until it tastes right." Ray's brother Tony, who was a cook in the military, also came to her rescue. Bernice now is a gourmet cook.

Another friend was Jack Quesnell. He was a varsity hockey player and had been a high school hockey player for Thief River Falls. He was in the seminary with Ray and me but left after the first year. He became a marriage counselor, and he and his wife, Alice, ran the

Pre-Cana course for years in the Twin Cities for people getting ready for marriage in the Roman Catholic Church.

While in college, Jack invited us to Thief River Falls for a visit. We had a great time. As we were driving to a dance one evening, I had a pint of whiskey, and I braggingly said when we drank, we threw away the cap. On the way home much later, one of our friends, Fran Bruggman, pulled out a quart of whiskey and said when we drank, we threw away the cap. We all had had too much to drink already, but to save face, we all five took a pull on the bottle trying to finish it.

Earlier, we had come to the dance and found we had to show identification and pay a cover charge. Of course, we all had fake IDs. One of us, Charlie, was over twenty-one. He had been in the navy and played trumpet in a band. He was also the only black man for miles around in Northern Minnesota. In the parking lot, we discussed strategy. I would take Charlie's ID and go in and check it out. As I returned, my report was positive. There were more girls than guys, so we were in business. We were far from the seminary, so what happens in Thief River Falls, we thought, stays in Thief River Falls. As we entered the hall and paid our cover charge, our fake IDs were no problem, except for Charlie. The bouncer looked at his card and said, "I just had a guy come in with this same name." We quickly got lost in the crowd. Charlie calmly showed the guy his ID picture and said, "You see any other black guy in here?" The bouncer looked closely at the picture, swallowed, and let Charlie pass.

For sleeping, we had to double up, and I got Charlie. As we were in bed, Charlie said he wanted to snuggle up to me. I told him he should get married. But he got close to me, and I thought if he tried anything, I would let him know quickly that he was out of line. At the time, my thinking was, he was black; and if I moved out of his way, he would feel rejected. He did not try anything, but years later, he became a Christian brother and taught at a number of Catholic high schools and received a number of awards for his work with youth. Then young people began to come forward accusing him of molesting them. He is now retired and living somewhere in Chicago. I remember, in the seminary, he said he had trouble with Latin and Greek and was leaving. I told him maybe he should look into being a Christian brother where Latin and Greek would not be a problem. I had no other encounter with him, so I always thought he was just a lonely person. I had no idea he would become a predator for teenage boys. In 2003, he was named in a suit charging that he molested a student in California back in 1982. That case was settled out of court for 1.1 million dollars. The latest count is nineteen cases against him.

I have to say that he never touched me in a sexual way, but as I look back, it looks like it was a warning of things to come. Perhaps if he had tried something, I could have put the word out, and I could have stopped him from becoming a Christian brother and molesting so many students. In our day, maybe nothing would have been done anyway. People did not understand pedophilia.

At the end of each summer after working construction, I used to take two weeks off before school started and go on vacation someplace. In 1956, Charlie invited us down to Houston, Texas. Another classmate went with me. We stayed with Charlie's family in the black community and went to all the black restaurants and bars. We were the only two white kids in the places. We were Charlie's friends and were more than welcome. One time, on the bus, I sat down in the front seat. Charlie said to come to the back of the bus with him. I said no. Charlie said if I was his quest, I should do what he said and not try to crusade because I would be leaving, and he had to still live here. I moved to the back of the bus.

Charlie also took us into Nuevo Laredo, Mexico. In the bar, we were approached by the "B" girls to buy them a drink. Then they wanted us to go in the back room for a little extracurriculum. I thought if I was in the seminary, I either had to be true to myself or be two-faced. The other guy with us said he would if I would. I do not use his name because he did become a priest, and later in his work, he was accused of molesting a teenage boy. He is no longer active in public ministry. I told him my thinking, and he shut up. Charlie just laughed. We had a few drinks and went back to Houston. As I look back on Charlie and my other friend, I had no idea that they would end up the way they did. I even had Charlie carry the processional cross in 1966 at my father's funeral. I simply thought they were men like me and would have to make their own decisions in life. They chose the wrong decisions.

My friend Fran Bruggman was on the wrestling team with me. He weighed in at 127 pounds dripping wet. He was a good wrestler and had gone to St. John's Preparatory High School, so he had more experience on the mat. He lived down a gravel road from St. John's University on a farm. As I got to know him as a friend, he would bring me over to his farm. Because we were freshman, as I mentioned, we were not allowed to have cars on campus. I had the bright idea to ask Fran if I could park my 1951 Ford behind a shed on his farm. His family had no problem with it, so we could use it on our free time. Fran didn't know how to drive, so I taught him on the gravel roads. He quickly learned all my bad habits, and he would race down the road and slide around the corners. I had to tell him he had to cool it more, or my car would blow up.

Christmas our sophomore year, I was home for Christmas vacation when I got a call from Fran's sister Ann. She was a couple of years younger than us but was a real beauty, so my ears perked up when she told me who she was. I thought maybe she needed a date for school and thought of me. I soon sank in my chair as she told me Fran had been in a toboggan accident and hit his head on a rock and was killed. Apparently, there were a number of open dirt spots on the hill, and the toboggan hit one of them, and Fran was tossed out and hit his head and was killed immediately. She asked if I would be a pallbearer. I swallowed hard and told her I would be honored. The funeral home was in Avon, five miles from St. John's. At the visitation, Charlie was very emotional. As we left, he walked down the main street calling out Fran's name. I think he felt he was in New Orleans, except he did not have his trumpet.

After the funeral we went to Fran's family farmhouse for lunch. I had one helping of everything. When they asked me if I wanted more, I politely said no. I had to watch my weight for wrestling. Ann was standing by the table, and she came over to me and whispered in my ear, "You remind me of somebody."

At 127 pounds, Fran had to have watched his weight. As she touched my ear, I thought it felt so good maybe I should drop out of the seminary and get married someday.

Fran's mother told me that Fran's high school ring was missing, and if I could look for it, she would appreciate it. At wrestling practice, I looked in the carry-on bag for the team. Searching the bottom thoroughly, I felt the ring. I proudly went to the Bruggman home with the ring. Mrs. Bruggman thanked me profusely and began to cry. Tears come to my eyes even now as I write this. We live in Avon in the summer, and as I show people the cemetery where all the monks are buried, I try to stop by Fran's grave and say hello. Why did he die at nineteen, and I am eighty plus?

Tom looking like the revolutionary,
Che Guevara, at the Elk's youth camp.

Ray Monsour and I worked two summers at the Elks Youth Camp on Big Pelican Lake in Brainerd, Minnesota. Our friend Jack Quesnell was the assistant director, so he hired us—we jokingly said—to do all the jobs he didn't want to do. We worked teaching swimming, took the kids hiking, sang around the campfires, ran arts and crafts, umpired baseball games, and everything else, as you could imagine. The kids were from seventeen down to twelve. They lived in cabins, as did we. Each night, we would tell them ghost stories to help them go to sleep and have nightmares. If they heard any noises, we would tell them they were Ray's camels walking around the woods. Kids would write home and tell their parents that there were camels in the woods. Ray, being Lebanese, claimed to keep his camels out of sight during the day. Some parents believed it. We also had to get some of the kids up each night so they would not wet the bed.

The camp ran for two weeks, and then another group would come in. The kids, for the most part, were underprivileged.

One day, as a new group came in from Duluth, the bus was followed by a highway patrol car. One of the kids had held up the bus station before the bus left the depot. We didn't work any magic on him as he was taken away.

One kid we did help was born with a deformed arm. He was a big kid, and to save face, he was a bully. Nobody dared make fun of his arm. His good arm with all the muscle looked like one of Popeye's. At swimming lessons, he claimed he couldn't swim because of his arm. Ray and I taught him the sidestroke and the backstroke, and he turned into one of our better swimmers. When we took him to the baseball field, he said the same thing. He could not play because he only had one arm. We told him about Pete Gray who played for major league baseball for St. Louis Browns in 1944. He had one arm also. He caught the ball in his glove hand and tucked the glove under his stump and threw the ball as well as anybody. He batted one-handed and hit line drives all over the field. We taught our guy the same options, and he was one of the first people chosen when we set up the teams. His parents at the end of the two weeks said he was a different son. He no longer needed to be a bully, and he was well-liked by all the other campers.

I ran a wrestling program and told the kids if they could stay with me for one minute, they could win five dollars. No one took any money off me. I only wished I could have done better at St. John's University, but with the knee and my one year of experience, I was limited to a backup position.

I also ran a boxing clinic. Jack Quesnell came out one time advertising as the Phantom and was challenging me. Jack was a great hockey player, but he wasn't a boxer, so I had to beat the Phantom (assistant director), which amused the campers.

Because the camp ran for two weeks, a new group of campers came in. However, the menu stayed the same. On a regular basis, we had hot dogs, beans, and potato chips. Can you imagine eating the same thing over and over again all summer? To this day, Ray and I won't eat a hot dog if we can help it. If we are forced to eat one to be sociable, we will smother it in onions and relish. We will also cut one up and put it with other things.

Every two weeks, Ray and I would receive our paychecks; and on Saturday, we would head into the Nisswa liquor store to cash it. Of course, we would have to have a drink or two with the locals. We were known as "the beards." Ray looked like Fidel Castro, and I looked like Che Guevera. The only problem we had was we were only eighteen years old, but we looked like we were in our twenties. The locals knew we worked at the Elk's camp on Big Pelican Lake, which served boys who were underprivileged, so often we didn't even have to pay for our drinks.

One time, there was a new bartender. As we asked to cash our two-week checks, he asked for identification. Now, we had our driver's license, but that would show that we were underage. You had to be twenty-one to drink in Minnesota. We told him we worked at the camp and did not bring any ID with us. We worked in the woods all week and did not carry any unnecessary items in our pockets. He said no ID, no cashing of checks. Ray and I looked at each other and thought, *What do we do now?*

One of the locals asked what was the matter. When we told him, he said, "These are the beards, and they work all week with troubled kids. They come in here every two weeks for a break and cash their meager checks, and you are not going to help them?" The answer was no. The locals looked at one another and said, "You don't serve them, we all walk!" At that, the whole group got up and started for the door. The bartender quickly said, "Hold it. Give me those checks, and what will you have?" We never had any problem after that.

One other time, we were in Brainerd on the weekend, and there was a professional wrestling match scheduled for that evening. Chief Don Eagle was taking on Harold "the Stone" Mason in the main event. We were early, so we walked around and talked to a few people. It seems they needed a referee for the final match of the evening. I told them I wrestled for St. John's University, and I could help them out. I was on. As the two wrestlers came to the middle of the ring, I told them, "Let's put on a real good match and no faking."

Chief Don Eagle stepped back and told the audience, "Now I fight two white men. Harold the Stonehead Mason and the referee." He put me right into the act. They proceeded to wrestle and do their acrobatics and take turns putting the other guy on the mat. I finally had to count to three when the good guy pinned the bad guy. We were in redneck territory, so the Native American lost again—so much for my efforts to have a real wrestling match.

One of the final events we had at the camp was a talent show. The campers would show their stuff and put on skits. Some of them made fun of the staff. The staff would join in and do their own thing. Ray Monsour and I would get up and start singing a camp song. Ray was not a singer. We called him Raymond "One Note." The joke was, I would stop singing and tell Ray he was off pitch. After a few times, he would pretend to get mad and stomp off. We always said you had to watch out for the "Mad Arab." The kids would laugh, and the show would go on. A few minutes later, Ray would appear and say he was tired of being made fun of with his singing. He would pull a gun (blank) and shoot at me. The lights would go out, and everybody would be screaming. The lights would go on again, and I would be at the front of the stage holding my chest. I had some ketchup in my hand, and I would smash it on my shirt so it looked like he hit me and I was bleeding. I would stumble a bit and then hit the floor. The kids were in a panic, and then I would get up, and Ray and I would put our arms around each other and have a good laugh.

The kids would be relieved, and it was on with the show. We would do our routine every two weeks until, one time, an older member of the Elks was visiting during the talent show. When we did our stick, he thought it was real, and he had a heart attack. He recovered, but our act got the hook. We wouldn't even think about doing something like that today.

At the end of the camping season, we decided to have a staff party. Raymond "the Arab" Monsour said he would host the event at his mother Sadie's, house on the west side of St. Paul. We made sure it was the famous Lebanese barbecue called La Ha Mishua. Yes, it would be lamb, beef, and chicken on the outside grill along with salad called slouta, Lebanese flat bread, cousa (zucchini stuffed with rice and beef), grape leaves stuffed with ground beef, and kibi (raw and cooked ground beef, with spices and pine nuts). We would have beer, soda pop, and of course, udda (pure grape, one-hundred-proof liquor) and baklava for dessert.

The two young counselors were bringing their girlfriends. Bob was dating a girl named Penny, and Bill was coming with Barbara. Barbara would later win the Ms. Minnesota contest.

Bob's nickname was "the Deacon." Bob was Jewish, but he loved to wear one of our old seminary wide-brimmed black hats, and he wanted to be called "the Deacon." So everybody called him Deacon. Bob's father was the liquor distributor for Seagrams in Minneapolis.

Bill wanted to be called "Shanks." He was tall and lanky and fit the name.

We decided we would pull a trick on the two girls. I had a full beard with long black hair. I put on raggedy pants with suspenders and a plaid shirt. I wore little round glasses and walked with a cane for effect. I had an old cap with a small bill. I looked like a bum from the word go. I planted myself in downtown Minneapolis in the park across from the main post office. The Shanks was driving. He had picked up Barbara in Bloomington and drove into Minneapolis to catch Penny and the Deacon. As they drove by the post office, Deacon said he had to mail a letter for his father.

The timing was perfect. I saw their car and made my way across the street in time to catch the Deacon returning to the car. I stopped him and said I needed a ride to St. Paul to my sister Sara's house. I said, "She takes care of me when I get this way." The girls were staring at me and knew I was under the influence of liquor. They told the Deacon to get in the car. The Deacon said, "Did you say St. Paul? Well, hop in. We're going that way."

He got in the back seat, and I opened the door and got in the front seat. The girls were stunned. Barbara moved as close to Shanks as she could get. I told them my name was Sammy Anderson from Stockholm, Sweden, and I tried to shake hands with Barbara and Shanks. Barbara reluctantly took my hand and released it as fast as she could. Shanks quickly took my hand over Barbara and shook it and said how happy he was to meet me. The Deacon did the same from the back seat, and Penny matched Barbara's quick, polite move.

Shanks took off, and we were on our way. I immediately took out my hip flask and took a drink. I told them how great America was and how friendly the people were, especially the young people. I offered them a drink to show my appreciation. Barbara declined, but Shanks took a swig and passed it back to the Deacon. He did the same, but Penny smiled and said she did not drink.

"Smukke damer," I said. "That means 'pretty girls' in Swedish."

The girls smiled and accepted the compliment.

"You people are great," I said. "And this calls for a new chew of tobacco."

I took a piece of wax paper out and put the old chew in it and put it in my top pocket. I took my pouch of Beechnut tobacco out and put in a new pinch. I offered it to Barbara, and she weakly said no. Shanks took a little, and so did the Deacon. "We have to be sociable," the Deacon said with a straight face.

I took my red handkerchief out from my back pocket and blew my noise. "I can't believe how nice you all are. Only in America can this happen. It almost brings me to tears."

I then took my cane, and with my fist, I knocked on my left leg. "It's wooden," I said. "I lost it in the big one World War Two." The tap on the leg bone sounded like it was wooden.

Now the girls were beginning to warm up to me a little. "Were you injured in battle?" Penny said in concern.

"Well, I fell off the back of a convoy trunk near our base. I was on my way back to camp, and I guess I had too much of the German beer," I confessed.

The girls looked at each other and rolled their eyes. There goes their hero, they thought.

We were approaching St. Paul's west side, and I spotted the Anchor Inn. "My sister lives right up here," I said.

Shanks pulled over in front of the bar. As I was getting out, I was thanking them again profusely. But then I put the touch on them. "Can you spare a few dollars? I don't want to go into my sister's empty-handed."

Shanks and the Deacon each gave me a couple of dollars. The girls were all smiles as they said goodbye. I turned and went right into the Anchor Inn.

I heard Barbara say, "Oh no, he went right into that bar."

In the bar I saw two of Ray Monsour's friends, Dick and Billy, leaning on the bar. When they saw me, they came over and said, "We don't want your kind in here."

I laughed and said, "It's me, Tanose. We just got back from the Elks Camp, and we are pulling a trick on a couple of the girlfriends of the younger counselors. I am dressed up like a bum, and I am on my way over to Sadie Monsour's for our staff party."

They laughed and bought me a beer. I often wondered what would have happened if I didn't identify myself.

Sadie's house was only two blocks from the bar, so I walked over there; and as I approached, the girls screamed, "There he is, Sammy Anderson!" They had been talking about me.

I came to the gate of the fence and started to open it. The joke was not over yet. Ray's older brother Joe was walking the perimeter of the fence with his large black Labrador dog Sahadah (which means 'flower' in Aramaic). He was dressed in his army fatigues with a gun visible on his hip, and he didn't look up to acknowledge anybody until I came to the gate.

"You, get the hell out of here, you goddamn bum," he shouted.

I opened the gate and came into the yard. Joe told Sahadah to "sig" me. Sahadah knew me, so I was confident he was not about to attack me. As I raised my cane to pretend I was going to hit the dog, Joe said, "No, you don't," and shot at me. Joe had blanks in his gun and was part of the hoax. I went down on the gravel driveway and twitched a couple of times and then lay silent.

"I thought I shot over the son of a bitch's head. I must have hit him," Joe moaned.

The girls were screaming and ran into the house, up the stairs, and Sadie found them huddled in the bathtub holding on to each other. Sadie was in on the whole thing, so she tried to calm the girls down. It took her about ten minutes to convince them it was just Tanose, and it was all a joke. They had heard about me and the camp from their boyfriends, so they finally came down and joined the party. From that point on, all had a good time; but every once in a while, I would see one or other of the girls taking a long look at me.

The whole idea of Sammy Anderson came from an experience Ray and I had as we were driving in St. Paul one day. We actually picked up a hitchhiker, and his name was Sammy Anderson. He pulled some of the same tricks I later did. Although, one of the things he did was spit his tobacco on Ray's pants. He was drunk, and we took him to his sister's place and had a good laugh about it. Little did we know that we would one day use his routine on two unsuspecting girls.

Ray and I were finishing our sophomore year at St. John's, and I thought I would go into regular college and leave Anselm Hall. I would take the same classes as the seminarians and graduate in philosophy and then decide if I wanted to go to the major seminary in St. Paul.

Ray found out he would have to take a different route. The former archbishop of the Archdiocese of Minneapolis and St. Paul, John Gregory Murray, had told Ray he couldn't study to be a priest there because he was from the Maronite Rite. The archbishop did not want to upset the patriarch from Detroit. But Archbishop Murray died, and the new archbishop William O. Brady told Ray he would be accepted as a candidate for the Minneapolis/St. Paul Archdiocese. It meant Ray would be going down starting his junior year in college. My classmates from Nazareth Hall would be coming over from the minor seminary too. I decided I might just as well go down to the major seminary with Ray. There was still the possibility that if I did go, I would be accepted, even with the history of having been kicked out of Nazareth Hall two years ago.

As it turned out, it looked like I could not take the seminary classes at St. John's anyway, unless I was actually in the seminary proper in St. Cloud diocese. Today that would be different. We could go to divinity school at St. Thomas University for two more years of college and then go to the major seminary. It would have saved us from going right back into the strict seminary routine.

Ray and I had another hurdle, and that was an entry test which included Greek. Ray was an excellent student in history, but he did not like Greek and was worried that the test might exclude him. My classmates from Nazareth Hall came through for us. They said they had four passages from the New Testament in Greek, and the test would be on one of those passages.

Ray and I went out each day at St. John's and walked in the woods. We joked about being behind the pine curtain, as opposed to the iron curtain, but it was a good way to memorize the four passages.

When we went down to St. Paul and took the entrance test, they passed the Greek component out, and Ray and I looked at it, and I mouthed over to him, "Bingo." There was one of the New Testament passages in Greek we had memorized. We wrote it out in a hurry and smiled through the rest of the test. We passed with flying colors. We were now headed to the St. Paul Major Seminary.

Chapter 3

The Saint Paul Major Seminary

The St. Paul Seminary, School of Divinity, and St. Thomas University came from the same roots. In 1885, Archbishop John Ireland founded St. Thomas Aquinas Seminary as a high school, college, and seminary. In 1894, a separate six-year seminary opened its doors. The seminary was built and endowed by the Methodist millionaire railroad magnate James J. Hill. He presented it as a gift to the Archdiocese of St. Paul and Minneapolis in honor of his Catholic wife, Mary Meheagan Hill. He financed and supervised the construction of six buildings, but it was the vision and leadership of Archbishop John Ireland that defined the traditions and set the standards for the seminary.

"Nothing short of the best and the highest is worthy of the priesthood and the causes which the priesthood represents," he wrote.

In 1987, the Archdiocese of St. Paul and Minneapolis, the University of St. Thomas, and the St. Paul Seminary joined together and once again established one School of Divinity. It now educates men for the priesthood and laymen and women for a number of other roles in the church. Although I call myself a Johnnie from St. John's University, I also claim that I finished my last two years of college under the eye of St. Thomas University.

In our day, the fall of 1957, things were a little different. The St. Paul Seminary was an entity onto itself. We did not attend any classes at St. Thomas. We had our own teachers and a few lay teachers for science and speech. For the most part, the professors were old and should have been retired. They read from books as their lectures. It was boring, but if you wanted to be a priest, that was what you had to put up with each day. You were discouraged from asking any questions because the Catholic Church already had all the answers, so it was not necessary to go any further.

As first year philosophy majors, we were assigned to one of the residential buildings called Cretin Hall. There were two other residential buildings called Loras Hall and Grace Hall, named after former archbishops. After two years of philosophy, we earned a bachelor of arts degree, plus a teaching degree. We then had four more years of theology to look forward to. Six years at the St. Paul Major Seminary was like doing hard time in a maximum prison. If you could put up with all the rules and boring lectures for that length of time, you had a good chance of becoming a priest. We had a number of strange-acting seminarians, but as long as they kept their nose clean, they would be moved along the way.

In the residence hall, we had accommodations composed of what was called an inner and an outer room. They were supposed to be an inner sleeping room made up of a bed, dresser, and closet.

The outer room was made up of a desk and chair for study. Because of the crowded conditions at that time, we had one person sleep and study in the inner room and the other person sleep and study in the outer room. That's right—the person in the inner room had to go through the other person's room to get out to go to the common bathroom down the hall or any other reason to leave the room. So much for privacy.

The schedule for the normal day was 6:00 a.m., wake up and get ready for meditation at 6:30 again if you could keep awake. Mass at 7:00 a.m. was followed by breakfast. We did fast from midnight till 7:30 when we literally broke our fast and ate. The food was cooked by a group of nuns and laywomen and girls. The nuns lived in the same refectory building, and the food was tolerable.

The Schedule

Classes started at 9:00 a.m. and went to noon. After lunch, we again had class from 1:00 to 3:00 p.m. Free time was from 3:00 to

4:30 p.m. We then had a spiritual talk and went to dinner at 6:00 p.m. Free time went until 7:30 p.m., when we had the sacred study time until 9:00 p.m. We then went to bed.

Once a week, we had a lecture by the rector of the seminary on rules and other matters. On Wednesdays and Saturdays, we had free time after lunch until 3:00 p.m. That time was for business like doctor's or dentist's appointments. You had to check out and check in on time or suffer the consequences.

Free time during the week included intramurals, which had teams chosen by the residents for football (touch), baseball, softball, basketball, and hockey. There was handball, tennis, cards, or just walking around the perimeter. In each season, I played every sport. You had to kill the boredom.

In the morning, our meditation consisted of a spiritual thought from the priest of the building. When he was done, most of us closed our eyes and caught a little power nap.

Our first-year dean was a priest named Ladislaus Sledge. The story was, he was smuggled out of Latvia in a potato sack to escape the communists. He called me in right away and told me he would be watching me very closely because I had been kicked out of Nazareth Hall two years ago. That made me feel real welcome. He would be on me like a tattoo. Great!

Classes

Most of the classes were taught by priests. They were older than the hills, and as I said, many read from their notes for their lectures. Our logic and metaphysics teacher was an exception, but most of us didn't know what he was talking about anyway. The history professor was so old he sat up in a chair in the aula, a large room with a stage, and he droned on about history, some of which he had lived through himself. I was serious and sat in front to hear him better, but it was difficult.

One time, a student cooked hot dogs during history class and sold them to the other students. I guess the old professor could not see to the back of the great aula.

In moral theology class, the professor read from his book and looked like a rabbit. We called him "Pinky," but not to his face. One day, he told us we would be talking on sexuality. He said we should be in our black cassocks, white surplices, and have a lighted candle. We didn't, but he said it was so sacred maybe we should. I couldn't believe it when he told us the body had decent parts, less-decent, and indecent parts. I thought God created the whole body as a temple of the Holy Spirit. We couldn't challenge him or ask any questions. I remember one tough kid from Chicago went up after class and privately asked him if married people could practice oral sex. "Pinky" fell off his chair. He told him that the final act had to be normal intercourse.

In dogmatic theology, we called the priest "Butch" behind his back. He sat like a toad behind his desk. Again, he would tolerate no questions. I finally got up my courage and asked him a question.

"Father, after the resurrection, how come Mary Magdalene didn't recognize Christ right away?"

He said, "Do you think you are the first one to ask that question?"

I said, "No, but there must be a reason."

He said Jesus had a glorified body, and it caused Mary to not see him as she knew him. My classmates froze and told me afterward that I was taking my life in my hands, and Butch would remember me at the next faculty meeting. He may have been one of the people who wanted to clip me later as a wise guy again.

The spiritual director was also from the last century. We called him "Curly" because he was bald, and each day, we had to sit in the big aula and listen to him drone on and on. Most of the professors should have been in a retirement center. We did have a breath of fresh air when two lay teachers came along. One was Bill Curtis, who taught us homiletics. He tried his best to improve the sermons, but when the focus was on the liturgy as doing the whole job, we were not encouraged to be like Bishop Fulton Sheen. It was held against us if we got too animated. The thinking was, the liturgy spoke for itself, and the church did not need any innovators to make it more interesting.

The other lay teacher was Dr. Geison from St. Thomas University. He taught biology. His famous saying was how difficult it was to give birth. "Have you ever tried to shit a football?" he said.

The rector, shortly after we got there, was transferred to a parish. His replacement, however, was the former rector at the minor seminary Nazareth Hall. I was seeing déjà vu all over again. Remember, we called him Big Lou. He was six feet five and had been a minor league baseball pitcher as a young man. The only thing that saved me was the fact he had been in the TB sanitarium when I was kicked out. So he had done nothing to expel me, and to his credit, he never hung it over my head.

There were the six buildings James J. Hill donated consisting of two residence halls (one more was added later): the administration building, which also served as the living quarters for the priests; the power house, which included a gymnasium; the refectory for meals; and the aula, which had most of the classrooms on the first floor; and the aula on the second level. The top floor of the aula was one big room for spiritual lectures, the rector's presentations and the history classes, plays, and other programs for all the seminarians at once.

The Chapel and Confession

The chapel was a beautiful building that had a main altar in front, and each side of the main aisle were seats for prayer, singing, and attending Mass. We faced one another and had to turn to see the altar. The two side aisles had small altars for the priests to say their daily Mass again to get the stipend. There were confessionals in the back. The spiritual director heard confessions each morning. It was always an awkward thing to see a couple of your classmates lining up for confession. What could they have done? Rob a bank? You suspected it was a tough night, and they gave in to impure thoughts and/or masturbation. Otherwise, they could have waited for the weekly confession. The system tried to keep the population from impure thoughts and acts. After all, we knew we would have to be celibate, and we might as well get used to it.

Each week, a few outside priests came to campus to hear confessions. We were supposed to pick one confessor and tell him your name as you came into the black box. He then could give you consistent spiritual advice. I had a good confessor by the name of Father Richard Moudry. He was our dean back in the minor seminary our freshman year, if you recall. He was also still one of the good guys. He later became a monsignor, which in French means "my lord." It is one step below a bishop. We always kidded Ray Monsour as a priest and told him one day he might be called Monsignor Monsour. He just laughed.

Spiritual Direction

We were also expected to pick an individual spiritual advisor and meet with him on a regular basis. I never had a spiritual advisor until a new professor came on board. He was said to be an expert on marriage, and he ended up also teaching economics, which he knew nothing about. The fact that, as priests, we would be preparing people for the sacrament of marriage, we better have some idea what we were talking about. He was quick with a turn of a phrase and had little stories and quotes. He seemed like maybe someone I could finally choose as my spiritual advisor. Despite the fact that he came out to skate one evening with bells on his white skates, I decided to give him a shot. He never came out to skate after that first time. I went to him, and he had me come in once a week. He would feed me a couple of his ideas, and off I would go. After about four weeks, I knocked on his door for my regular meeting. He opened the door and told me my sermon was not ready yet, and I should come back later. I told him I was there for my spiritual-direction meeting and had no sermon. He said, "Oh!" and said I should come back next week. He didn't even remember my name after a month of visits.

Needless to say, I never went back—and so much for a personal spiritual director.

The Gym

Because the intramural programs and the handball courts could not accommodate all the students, we also had a weight room in the gym; and again, as in a prison, we could build up our muscle lifting weights. Ray Monsour and I would lift regularly until Ray told me my back was getting muscle-bound. I had to change my routine if I didn't want to look like Arnold Schwarzenegger.

We had to be our own referees in all the games, so if we called a foul in basketball, we may have had an enemy for months.

Walks

When we had free time and no scheduled sports, we could walk around the perimeter alone or with a friend. Of course, we had to be careful of a particular friendship, which we still didn't know meant a possible homosexual relationship. Nobody paid that much attention to us, so we, Ray Monsour and I, didn't get called on having a particular friendship.

On Wednesdays and Saturdays, when we went off grounds for a walk, we often ran into coeds from Macalester College. In the spring, some would wear shorts and a halter; and as they passed us by, they would giggle and often laugh out loud. Because, you see, when we left campus, we had to wear our black suits, white shirts, black ties, and wide-brim black hats. We looked like a cross between the Mafia and Hasidic Jews. Later, when I worked in New York City, I always had a special respect for the Hasidic Jews clothing. As we walked by the coeds laughing at us, I turned to Ray and said, "This is what it means when they say we are fools for Christ."

On campus, we had to wear long black cassocks. At High Mass, we wore a small hat called a biretta with three points you could use to take them off at different times during the ceremony to show respect. The points actually came about over the years of taking off the hat. They eventually made them with the three points to save us the trouble of wearing them to that design.

We often bought the clothes from the local Jewish tailor.

Because my dad was a police officer, I would get his hand-me-downs as far as white shirts go. They were frayed at the cuffs and the collar, but under a cassock, no one really noticed. However, with a black suit, the sleeves and collars stuck out. One time, Ray took me over to an older couple's home on one of our Wednesdays out, and they thought I was so poor that when I was ordained, they gave me twenty-five dollars. When I resigned six years later, they asked for their money back. I sent it to them.

Teaching and the FBI

After four years of college, we earned our teaching certificate by practice teaching at the Catholic grade schools in the Twin Cities. The principal, who was a nun, supervised us and approved our work for credit, and the State of Minnesota awarded us a certificate to teach in elementary and high schools.

We also went out to the west side of St. Paul and taught religion to the Mexican American children from Our Lady of Guadalupe parish. This was Ray Monsour's old stomping grounds on the west side, so he and I were put in charge of the teaching. Every Wednesday during the school year, we traveled over to the parish to teach. We went to the public school in the area and picked up the kids and walked them to the parish classrooms. Ray and I would pick up the absentee slips and assign our crew to a class. This was a plum job because, after class, we would go to Ray's mother, Sadie's, place, and she and her cousin Katie Deeb would feed us like kings. We could pick our own friends for the job. Obviously, everybody wanted to join our staff.

One day after teaching, Ray and I got called into the rector's office. We thought our jig was up. There in the office stood two men in suits. The rector "Big Lou" McCarthy said that these men were from the FBI, and we were accused of selling numbers on the west side. We explained that what we were collecting in the envelopes were the absentee slips. With our black suits and all, we certainly looked like the Mafia. The rector had a big laugh, and the men stayed sober-looking and wrote up our explanation and left.

Theater

In my years in the seminary, I tried to deal with the boredom by trying out for plays and acting or hamming it up, depending how one looked at it. At Nazareth Hall, I was one of the leads when I got slashed on the hockey rink the day of the performance. I had boarded a guy named Phil Byrnes, and he didn't like it. He kicked with his skates, and I said, "Watch out! You could cut someone!"

As I looked down, I saw blood. He had gotten me right above my skate and just under my shin guard. They rushed me to the hospital, and I was sewed up in no time. When I returned, Father Karl came to see me. He was the director of the play and was concerned that I would not be able to perform. I had one of the leads, so I think he had more worry about the play than me. I assured him that the play would go on. I didn't even limp that night. He taught German and was always late. As he came down the hallway to class, he would begin the Our Father in German and was half done by the time he entered the room. We would finish the opening prayer together.

At St. John's University, I tried out for the play *The Caine Mutiny Court-Marital*. I ended up as the understudy for Captain Queeg. I was only a freshman, so a senior got the part. I was the court stenographer. I remember Father Francis, the assistant dean of Anselm Hall, told me I had a clear, strong voice that everybody could hear. The monk who directed the play turned up on the list of priests who had sexually abused students. Maybe I was lucky to get a minor part that time.

At the major seminary, I was in a few plays also. One was *My Fair Lady*. Of course, we had no women actresses, so they changed the name of the play to *With a Little Bit of Luck*. The lead was a paperboy. I was cast as Mr. Doolittle. It was a musical, so I had to sing "Get Me to the Church on Time." In it, I had to sing the word *philandering*. Sure enough, I got called in by the rector "Big Lou" McCarthy for using the word. He asked me if I knew what it meant. I told him I did, but it was part of the song. He said, "I mean, good God, the nuns were there."

I looked at him and said the nuns are adults, and they should be able to handle it. He stifled a laugh and sent me on my way.

We had variety shows where we made fun of the faculty. One time, Ruf North, a good friend, and I did a comedy routine. Ruf was a year behind me in school. So as I got books from my older brother Ken (until he was kicked out), I would use them and then pass them on to Ruf, who would hand them down to my younger brother Ed. We had written many of the answers in the books over the years, so my brother Ed could benefit from our labors. Ed was already an A student, so he was that much further ahead of his classmates—a fact, you will learn later, led to his expulsion.

Yes, another Christian brother would be kicked out of the seminary. Where was the Holy Ghost when we needed his Spirit?

Ruf had the bright idea that in our comedy routine, we should do it in black face like Amos and Andy. We only had two black students in the whole school, so we went to them and asked if they would be offended if we did the black-face thing. We told them the jokes which were not racial, and they thought it would be hilarious. But this was 1961. We did two jokes we got from a friend of Ray Monsour's on the outside by the name of Doc Helsper.

When we walked out on stage, the student body went crazy. We told a few quick one-liners, and one of our jokes was on reincarnation. It involved Rodney and Reggie with British accents. I played the straight-man Rodney.

Ruf started as Reggie talking to Rodney. "I dare say, Rodney, do you believe in reincarnation?"

"Reincarnation?" said Rodney. "I don't even know if I can even spell it!"

"Well," said Reggie, "say you ups and dies. They plant you in the ground. Now you're part of the ground. Aren't you?"

"I guess I am," thought Rodney out loud.

"Now up pops a flower," said Reggie. "You were part of the ground, and now you are part of the flower, right, Rodney?"

"I guess you are right, Reggie", Rodney said, scratching his head.

"Along comes a cow, walking through the open gate, and stops and takes a bite of that flower. Now you were part of the ground, and now you are part of the flower and part of that cow. Do you follow, Rodney?"

"I follow," said Rodney as he slowly pointed out each step with his finger.

Reggie stated, "The cow sashays down the road, and all of a sudden"—Reggie made the sound of the cow dropping a cow pie— "Now you haven't changed much, have you, Rodney?" As Ruf said this, he moved his foot side to side as if he had just stepped in the cow pie.

The crowd went wild with laughter. Not only on the joke but also it was done in black face and a little off-color for a seminary.

Our last joke had Rodney and Reggie again in London at a private club. Reggie had been to Africa, so Rodney asked him if he hunted any lions. Reggie explained how he was out on a safari and came face-to-face with a male lion. The lion roared, and Reggie made a loud roar. He then said, "Oops, I did it again," Rodney said.

"What did you do?" asked Rodney excitedly.

"I loaded my pants," said Reggie.

"When the lion went *roar*?" said Rodney.

"No." Reggie squirmed. "When I just went roar."

Ruf and I went off to thunderous applause, patting each other on the back as we did the elephant walk side by side leaving the stage.

It didn't last long. The dean of Cretin Hall, my old spiritual director, must not have liked the imitation someone did of him in an earlier skit, and he made a federal case out of our black face. We explained to the rector that we had talked to the two black students, and they were okay with it. It made no difference. We were politically incorrect, and we had to admit it. It went into the snag book and would be discussed at the next faculty meeting.

I have always liked to act, and after I retired, I still get into the local variety shows and ham it up.

Kentucky

The bishop of Covington, Kentucky, had gone to the St. Paul Seminary when he was in school, so he sent many of his seminarians there also. The men from Kentucky wanted to make things a little easier for those who came after them, so they put together what was called "the Kentucky notes." This was all the notes one needed to take the tests at the end of a marking period. Of course, we all received copies of the notes, and that was what we memorized, and we easily passed the various tests.

One time, my roommate, whom we called "Honey Dew," decided he was going to do his own studying. Believe it or not, he was also from Kentucky. His answers were not like the Kentucky notes. He didn't pass. He quickly went back to the Kentucky notes and had no problem after that.

One summer, Ray Monsour and I decided we would end our summer and head down to Covington, Kentucky, and see two of our classmates. They took us to a bar that played country music. We were having a good old time drinking and enjoying the music. I made a request to have the band play "I Walk the Line" by Johnny Cash. The table next to us was talking loudly, so I turned to them and said could they hold it down a little because I wanted to hear my request. That didn't go over too well, and one guy told me to "kiss his ass." My quick response was to "bare it." He was up in a flash, and we were nose to nose. Someone grabbed me from behind in a full nelson. I proceeded to use my wrestling skills, and I rolled him over my shoulder, and he landed on the floor looking more than surprised. However, as he got up, he pulled a gun and pointed it right at me. He was the bouncer for the bar, I found out in a hurry. I put my hands up and said, "That's cool. I am just leaving." With a smile on my face like Richard Prior, I calmly walked to the door, always facing the bouncer. He let me walk out. Ray, meanwhile, was taking a short nap, but he woke up in a hurry and followed me out the door. Our classmates from Kentucky slowly followed us.

The next day at their church picnic in the local park, we learned that a week earlier, the bouncer had shot someone for much less than what I had done to him.

We had one more episode before we left. Some of the friends of our classmates decided to pull a trick on some of their other friends. They introduced Ray and me as foreign exchange students and told us to use our language skills to fool them into thinking we could not speak English but only foreign languages. Ray spoke his Lebanese, and I spoke German and French. We were both limited in our spoken words, but we pulled it off. I called the wise guy in the group Monsieur le Burr? He had a crew cut, so that was why I capped him Monsieur le Burr. After stringing him along for about an hour, we told him in clear English that it was good talking to him. He just about died, but his friends thought it was a great joke on a wise guy who deserved it.

Sandy, JFK, and the Lutheran Minister

In 1960, John F. Kennedy was running against Richard Nixon for the presidency of the United States. I still was playing summer softball for the Glass Stem, a bar in Bloomington, Minnesota. I had the brace on my left leg from my football injury back in 1956. As I stated before, I hurt my knee again playing softball and had to go into the hospital. They hauled me in a station wagon down to Abbot Hospital in Minneapolis. Bouncing around in the back of the vehicle was not my idea of a good time and taking one for the team. The doctor operated on me and cleaned up all the torn ligaments and cartilage. I was in the hospital for three days.

My loyal friend Ray Monsour visited me every day. He took a bus from St. Paul over to Minneapolis.

One of my nurses by the name of Sandy took good care of me also. She was a very attractive blonde, and she was very friendly and about my age. When she found out I was in the seminary, she really paid attention to my needs. She asked me about John F. Kennedy and the pope. She said her minister was Lutheran and thought JFK would be under the pope's thumb. I told her no such thing would happen. She suggested that when I was up and around, we should go down to Granite Falls, her hometown, and talk to her minister. I smiled and quickly agreed.

We drove down on a Saturday, and I spent two hours trying to convince him that JFK would serve all the people, and his being Catholic would not be a problem. I don't think he was too persuaded by my efforts.

Sandy was still mystified that I was willing to be a celibate priest. I gave her the line the priests gave us. We would be free to serve all the people and not have to have a wife and children prevent us from total dedication. I will respond to that idea later in this book.

I told Sandy if she thought my sacrifice was tough, she should see the monks up at St. John's Abbey. They lived in a monastery and said prayers at certain times of the day, and unless they were assigned to a special parish or teaching position, they all lived a celibate life behind the pine curtain.

Of course, I had to drive her up ninety miles from Minneapolis to see these unique people. This was a monastery. While as a secular priest like I was studying to be was out in the world trying to save everybody, these men lived in a closed setting away from the world and prayed for everybody. She wanted to see the monks for herself. We arrived in time to see the monks march in for evening prayer. Sandy's mouth dropped open. She couldn't believe that these people lived in a monastery and were celibate for life. I saw some of the monks look at us as they passed out of church back to their cells. I was hoping no one recognized me sitting there with a striking blonde. I never heard any comments from my friends in the monastery who knew me, so I guess I was still safe from causing any scandal.

It was summertime, and I was working for Raunhorst Construction Company. I couldn't believe it when they assigned me to work on St. Austin's Hall, a new building out at my old minor seminary, Nazareth Hall. They were getting a new gymnasium along with new classrooms, a refectory, and offices. The old gym was once a swimming pool, and it was covered over, and a floor was installed. However, one end was short; and if you tried a layup, you had to stop quick or run into the wall. It reminded me of our old gym back at St. Peter's in Richfield. It was really a refectory, so the ceiling was low, and we had to shoot our basketball on a line drive or hit the ceiling.

Our home in Richfield was about ten miles from Nazareth Hall, which was on 3003 North Snelling Avenue in Roseville. I made it a point—because it was on the way home from work—to drive past the nurses' quarters in Minneapolis to see if I could spot Sandy walking to or from work. I figured if I did, maybe God was telling me to quit the seminary and get married, if not to Sandy, maybe to some other person I could begin dating. Sandy's boyfriend was in the military, so I guess she used me as a distraction until he got out.

When I got back to school, Sandy introduced me on a Saturday to her boyfriend, Tom, and I played handball with him at the University of St. Thomas. I beat him. He was a nice guy, but I thought I might have underestimated myself and should have pursued Sandy a little more. On another Saturday afternoon, we were walking over to play handball again, and Sandy was with us. She walked between us, holding us with each of her arms, and called us *her* "two Toms." I don't think her Tom appreciated it too much. I thought two Toms were one too many. They did get married, and they sent me an invitation. I could not go to the wedding because I was not allowed to leave the seminary to attend a wedding. I think the authorities of the church did not want me to see how happy the married couple was and me standing there as a future celibate, guessing what I was missing. I sent them a framed picture of a modern Jesus. I am sure they gave it to their church. The good thing in all of this was, John F. Kennedy got elected president of the United States, and the pope did not have a pipeline from the Vatican to Washington, DC.

Brother Ed

My brother Ed was in Nazareth Hall, the minor seminary, for the full six years. He now came into the St. Paul Major Seminary with me. I was in my first year of a four-year theology program. Ed was in first year of philosophy at Cretin Hall, and I was in Loras Hall. As I said, Ed was an A student, an excellent athlete, and all-around great seminarian. Many of his classmates were also top-notch candidates for the priesthood. In December, Ed got mononucleosis and had to go home to recuperate. I went to his philosophy teacher Father William (who we called "Bucky" because of his smile and big teeth) and asked for study material so Ed could keep up at home. He said Ed was an excellent student, so he should concentrate on getting well, and he would have no trouble catching up when he returned. He did make a dig about if it was me, he would have considered some homework.

Ed came back in January and not only caught up but led his class in the second semester.

During Good Friday that spring, Ed was cleaning his inner room with a dust mop and was listening to Burl Ives on his tape recorder when he heard Hank Christenson, his roommate, in the outer room, say, "Hello, Father."

Brushing past Hank and entering Ed's room came the dean of the building, Father John O. "Where is the woman?" he said. Ed informed him there was no woman in the room, but he did have his tape recording on, and Burl Ives did have a high-pitched voice. Ed's room was two floors above the dean's room, and the heating pipes ran from Ed's room down to the dean's rooms. Father O could hear voices above him. He ran upstairs, burst into the room, and began to look in the closet and under the bed. He tipped the mattress over and tore the sheets back. He then stomped out of the room. Ed and Hank looked at each other and held back a laugh. It turned out not to be a laughing matter.

Sometime later in the month, one of Ed's friends came down to his room to get the notes for metaphysics class. Ed always wrote an outline of the class material. Because most of the class didn't know what was going on, they depended on Ed to make sense of the lectures. Unfortunately, this was the sacred 7:30 to 9:00 p.m. study period, and there was to be no talking to other students. As Ed's classmate walked away with Ed's notes, Father O was also running up the steps to the second floor. He chewed Ed out for talking during this sacred time. Again, Ed shrugged it off and went about his business.

In June after finals, we were preparing to head out for summer vacation and summer jobs to make some money. As we sat in the refectory eating supper, the rector Big Lou had one of the faculty waiters sent down to have certain students come to see him after supper. This person, remember, was called the angel of death because it meant someone was going to be kicked out or put on the carpet for something.

The faculty ate on one level above the student body and looked down on us in more ways than one.

Ed was watching the angel of death coming down the aisle, thinking it was getting too close to his table. All of a sudden, the angel stopped in front of him. "The rector would like to see you in his office immediately after dinner." Ed froze. Seven years of a good record in the seminary with an A average couldn't be a problem, he thought. His table joked that he should have put ketchup on his table leg like the Jews did in Egypt putting blood on their doors to keep the angel of death from coming in to take one of their family members away. It was our own Passover. Maybe the rector wanted to give Ed a job for next year. After all, he was assigned the job of official bell ringer back at Nazareth Hall.

The next thing I heard was that, sure enough, Brother Ed had been kicked out. "No one voted for you at the faculty meeting," Big Lou said. Ed was stunned. Apparently, the dean of his building—again, my old short-term spiritual director—recommended his expulsion. No one would go against a dean. Being sick with mono meant no one really got to know Ed. All the old-timer faculty rubber stamped a dean's word.

When I got the news, I was furious. This would be the third Christian brother to go. Ed was the smartest and the best of the bunch. My mother and dad would be bewildered. I decided I had to go see Big Lou myself. This was an injustice, and I was sure the Holy Spirit was not behind this. I knew if I didn't handle it diplomatically, I would be following Ed out the door. As I approached the administration building, my brother and good friend Ruf met me. Ed said, "Don't go into Big Lou's office." He had decided he was going to quit anyway. He had talked it over with his priest spiritual advisor and was not coming back after the summer. Ruf told me if I proceeded, I would be the next to go. I stepped back. Now I was all the more determined to keep a low profile and make it to the priesthood and change a few things in the Catholic Church.

Ed went on to St. Thomas University. They told him he had enough credits to graduate, but it would have to be in Latin or chant. He decided to take only political science classes and graduate with a degree in political science. He went to the St. Thomas University football coach and said he wanted to go out for the football team as a linebacker. The coach said, as a senior, it was not worth all the work to bring him up to par as a linebacker. He told the coach it was his loss. He went on to play touch football in a state league for Bloomington and was voted all-state.

He went on to the University of Minnesota Law School and went into practice in Bloomington, Minnesota. He ended up in his own very successful law practice. He was deputy chief of the Bloomington volunteer fire department. He is now retired and has three daughters and six grandkids. He still meets with a number of his old classmates from the seminary, some of whom were ordained and some were not. He says he does not regret the years he spent in the seminary because of his education and lasting friends.

A Sexual Attack

This is probably the hardest part to write about in my whole story. It points out clearly that the Catholic Church transferred priests from one parish to another and even from one diocese to another when there was substantial evidence that priests were involved in molesting young people.

This part of my story begins in the major seminary and is carried out into actual parishes. Was this because the hierarchy was protecting "Mother Church" from scandal and being sued, or was it also due to ignorance about pedophile behavior?

Many priests were sent away for treatment, but apparently, the professionals didn't understand pedophile behavior any more than the bishops because they often sent the patient right back to the diocese as ready to go back to serving as priests. They apparently did not know that, like alcoholism, pedophile behavior will not stop because they went through some counseling. It is an addiction. Pope Francis said he learned the hard way. On appeal, he let a priest back into ministry after being told he was cured from molesting victims. The person went back into his old behavior. The pope now says no more appeals in proven cases of molestation.

Well, here goes my experience.

In 1960, I was in the second year of a four-year theology course. I was assigned to Grace Hall with a roommate who had been in the seminary for over five years. I will not mention his name, even though in the future he will be listed in three public newspaper accounts of sexual abuse from three different Minnesota dioceses. This means he acted out in all three places. He also passed away on November 4, 2004, so he is no longer acting out.

Because we were given rooms often alphabetically, Tom Christian was paired with the next person in alphabetical order. I did not have a choice of roommates. This person was born on October 10, 1936. That made him one year older than I was. John Doe or JD is what I prefer to call him. I do not want to use his real name. He has since passed away, so I will leave it that way. He will not abuse another individual. JD was a tall, thin man and wore his cassock as tight as he could. He also used cologne heavily. His father was black, and his mother was white. But JD was very sensitive about his mixed race. One of his friends from the seminary received a black doll in his home mail one summer stating, "This is your friend JD."

In the late '50s, there was a lot of racial tension building across the country. We had seminarians from Kentucky who believed separate but equal was still the way to go. It took two to three years for them to start thinking any other way.

JD was treated well by all our classmates, but he still was overly sensitive about his mixed race and had a loud laugh whenever he was uncomfortable. He often told people he was part Hawaiian to distract them from his short curly hair and distinct black features. He had a rather light complexion. He was always asking questions about circumcision and acted naive about sexual matters. One time, in his pajamas, he showed me his penis and said, "Look what that doctor did to me." He was black-and-blue from an adult circumcision. That explained his questions on circumcision. I was always uncomfortable when he asked these types of questions, but I thought he was sincere, overly protected, and didn't know about things, and I tried to bring him into the real world.

He knew I wrestled in college and asked me to teach him some holds. I hesitated but thought he needed some masculine blood in his system. So we went over to St. Thomas University and used their wrestling mats. JD was strong but awkward, and when he put his hands on me, I really felt uncomfortable. I gave him one lesson and then said that was enough. He had the general idea and didn't need to learn anymore.

When we were assigned rooms, he was in the inner room, and I had the outer. We all had to go down the hall to go to the bathroom, shower, shave, wash up for bedtime, and brush our teeth. JD would wait in his room and time his leaving for the bathroom just as I was undressing and putting on my pajamas. I got so I would fake getting undressed by dropping my shoes and then just sitting on my bed fully clothed until he went by.

One evening, I had a bad cold and was coughing into the night. All of a sudden, he was standing next to my bed with an electric lantern. He said he couldn't sleep with my coughing even though there was a closed door between us. He said he had some Vicks vapor rub, and he would put it on my chest. As he attempted to open my pajama top, I pushed his hand away and told him to go back to bed. If I wanted any Vicks, I would put it on myself. He reluctantly went back to his room.

The next day, I gave him a letter to type. He was an excellent typist. It was a letter I had been asked to write for the director of the Elk's Youth Camp that Ray Monsour and I had worked at that summer with our friend Jack Quesnell as assistant director. The director had been accused of tampering with a camper. The camper was a troublemaker nicknamed "Pickles." He said he was riding into town with the director and was touched inappropriately. The director asked me for a letter to his board of directors because I was in the seminary, and that might carry more weight. I wrote that the director was very friendly and had a great sense of humor but had never done anything in my two summers there that even came close to being inappropriate. The board of directors for the Elks' Youth Camp were ready to fire him. He was of retirement age, so he did retire.

After JD had typed my letter, I sat down with him and said that the director may lose his job over the accusation from the camper. I told him that what he did last night could be seen as a homosexual advance, and it was very inappropriate for him to try to rub Vicks on another man's chest. I again explained to him that I was capable of putting Vicks on my own chest. I told him that if he tried anything like that again, I would report him to the rector.

Two weeks later, I was walking up the steps to our second-floor room. He was walking down. I had been playing intramural football and had been kneed in the buttocks. In the seminary, touch football was one way to work off steam, and it was more like tackle football the way we played it. He wanted to know what happened, and I told him I was bruised up and patted my backside. Sure enough, that night, he appeared at my bedside with his lantern and wanted to rub Ben Gay on my backside. I couldn't believe it. I told him if he didn't leave, he should count his teeth because I would be knocking them all out. He grabbed my pajamas and pulled them down to my knees. My penis jumped, and he grabbed my pubic hair and pulled on it. "We have to stop that like this," he said and reached to grab my pubic hair again. I jumped out of bed and told him to get out or get hurt. He left. I slept with one eye open the rest of the night. I felt like I was almost raped. Here I was, an all-city and all-suburban midget football all-star, wrestler, boxer, hockey, track runner, and basketball player—and almost a victim of a sexual predator.

Now, how was I going to report him? My reputation as a tough guy might work against me. I went to JD's former roommates and asked them if they ever had any problem with JD. One person, his last roommate, John Conrad, and a good friend of mine, told me he would back me 100 percent if I went into the rector. Other classmates said they had experienced some of the same strange behavior as I had. They talked about JD coming through their rooms while they were undressing, and he asked the same questions about sex that he had asked me. It appeared he was getting off on talking about sexual matters. JD earlier talked to me about coming into a public restroom, and two men were playing with each other's genitals at the urinal. He was fascinated by the fact that they kept doing it for a long period of time. JD, I was convinced, fixated on sexual matters. There was now a pattern, and he was escalating his behavior. Other classmates told me they would back me too if I reported him. I was worried I would be kicked out with JD, and I wanted witnesses to collaborate my story.

I went to my confessor Father Dick Moudry, a good role model for all of us, and he told me to meet him in the administration building after all the confessions were heard. I explained the two encounters, and he told me to go tell the rector immediately.

As I explained the same story to Big Lou, he said, "Good God, what about the altar boys?" I knew what he meant.

Big Lou told me it was not my fault, and he would act on it immediately. JD was gone that afternoon. Unfortunately, Big Lou told him that the faculty had observed him over a period of time, and they did not think he was a proper candidate for the priesthood. He did not say anything about his behavior toward me. Maybe he was protecting me, but as you will see, it didn't work.

JD was a member of a local parish in Minneapolis. His pastor was an old respected priest, and when JD told him the seminary had told him he was no longer a proper candidate for the priesthood, the pastor went ballistic. Here, the parish was waiting for their favorite son to become a priest; and after six years in the seminary, he was being turned out. Big Lou told him the true facts, and the pastor went back to JD with the real reason and told him. All was quiet for the time being.

That Christmas, a short time after the encounter, I came home on vacation to find a bouquet of flowers on our dining-room table. It almost reached the floor on both sides of the table. The note said, "To Mommy and Daddy from Tommy." I always called my mother *mom* and father *dad*. I never used the name *Tommy*. I pulled my Dad aside and told him I did not send the flowers, and did he do this in my name? He said no. I quietly pondered the gift. I knew my parents were wondering, but I never said anything more to my mother.

When I got back to the seminary, I got the bill: seventy-five dollars. I went to Lund and Lang, the florist, and told them I did not order the flowers. But our family did get the benefit of the flowers, but they were charged on what was a credit card in my name, and I wanted to cancel that so no more purchases could be made. They were very understanding and said they would split the cost with me. I agreed and paid $37.50.

The next visiting Sunday, I told my mother and father about it and said it may be JD sending the flowers. He was involved in getting flowers for the church altar at the seminary and knew the routine. My mother's mouth dropped when I mentioned his name.

"Is he bothering you?" I asked.

"Yes," she said. He was calling her and telling her how terrible her son Tommy was for getting him kicked out of the seminary after six years. I almost blew a gasket. I told her if he called again, that we would call the police and have him charged with harassment. My mother never talked about it again, so I assume he did stop.

No one publicly told anyone about JD's behavior, and he took a job as a teacher in Minneapolis at an all-boys school (DeLaSalle). He also became the tennis coach and was known to push the boys against the lockers to discipline them. This event took place in 1960. It appears that people did not recognize that sexually acting out inappropriately was a pattern, and they figured to give JD a chance and not tell the principal at an all-boys school to be aware of JD's past behavior. They assumed he learned his lesson, and they did not want to ruin his chances of getting work.

Years later, in 1976, I was married and had two children and was living in Minneapolis and running a residential corrections program. I got a call from the vocations director from the Archdiocese of St. Paul and Minneapolis. He said JD was applying for admission into the seminary again. He told the vocations director that he had been dismissed in 1960 for getting in a fight with Tom Christian. The director knew me, and based on my boxing and wrestling background and my tough-guy reputation, he figured I would have killed JD in any kind of fight. I told him to stop over, and I would explain the true story to him, but not over the phone. He came, and I clued him in. He left, and I heard later that they were letting JD into the seminary again but up at St. John's Major Seminary, and he could study for the Duluth Diocese. They thought he was more mature now. He was ordained in 1980. He soon showed his true colors. A lady had died and gave her money to the local parish. JD was the assistant, and he put the money in his own personal account. He was caught and was also on the list for molesting underaged children. He was sent to the New Ulm Diocese. There, he was assigned to a priest who had cancer and needed help. In visiting a friend, I met the priest who had been assigned JD as an assistant. He told me the following story.

JD was preparing a couple for marriage and told the groom he was coming over to talk to him about some sensitive areas. He told the young man to go into the bedroom and take off his clothes so he could examine him before the wedding. The man told him to leave and reported him to the parish priest, who, in turn, reported him to Bishop Raymond Lucker. The bishop was a good man and told JD he would have to go for treatment. JD refused, so the bishop took him out of ministry.

Before he left New Ulm, the police caught JD in a motel room with an underaged minor boy. They did not prosecute and must have seen it as a church responsibility. JD left town. Not only were some of the hierarchy slow to respond to this type of behavior, but often, law enforcement were enablers too. He worked in a parking garage for a period of time and later was hired as a high school teacher in a Minneapolis suburb. No one told people ahead of him anything about his problem. When JD died, his obituary read that he died suddenly. It noted that he loved cooking and interior decorating and had many friends.

In the final section of this book, I would like to give my view on what the Roman Catholic Church did and did not do when a priest was identified as a molester.

Word from the Outside World

In the seminary, we had little word from the outside world. Some students hid small transistor radios and used the radiators as an antenna. If you were caught, you could be expelled. Television could be watched from 6:30 to 7:30 p.m. during the week, so if you were lucky, you might catch a little of the news. I decided that there had to be a better way. I talked to the janitor, who had his supply room and sitting area in the basement of Grace Hall. We had to walk right by his space to get to the pool and ping-pong tables on one end and the television on the other. He was an okay guy, so I asked him if I paid for the daily paper, he could read it and let me sit in and read it when he was out working. It worked for him. I had a couple of friends who joined in, and I collected a couple of bucks from them, and we had a deal.

One of the students was chosen on each floor of the residence buildings to be the resident prefect for the whole floor. One of my classmates (John Conrad, who has since passed away) was chosen, so I made an arrangement with him to hide a television set under his bed. Again, I bought an old TV on a Wednesday off campus and carried it back in a big cardboard box so no one knew what it was. I had a few other classmates go in on it, and we could watch TV when the coast was clear. That meant the dean of the building was gone, which was most weekends and a number of evenings. We tried to keep up to date as best as we could with what was happening in our world.

One other student had the same idea. He was the school photographer and set up a dark room to develop his pictures. He had a large box which stated, "Film in process. Do not open." Inside the box, he had his own television set.

Again, it made no sense to limit our contact with the outside world that we would soon be working with in a number of ways. Some of the seminarians never learned how to communicate well with women, much less problem people, but they kept all the rules and were ordained.

Languages

We studied many languages in the course of twelve years in the seminary. Latin was the big one. Today the priest says Mass and reads their prayers in their native language. I can't count the number of seminarians who quit over the years because they could not master Latin.

I also took German, French, Greek, Hebrew, and Spanish. I can still hardly laugh in English. Latin helps me tell my wife certain words for her crossword puzzles or questions on *Jeopardy*. I suppose the other languages come up on occasion, but I cannot speak more than a few words in any of them. *Repetitio est mater studiorum*—"Repetition is the mother of all learning." I use that once in a while along with *mirabile dictum* ("marvelous to say").

We took Spanish once a week for a semester after supper. It was not enough. If I could go back, I would take only Spanish and spend a summer or two in Mexico or Spain and try to become fluent. I could have used that often in my work as a priest and later as a criminal justice specialist. As a teenager, I even worked alongside migrant workers on the farms in Minnesota.

Titsie Flies

I rarely got to serve as a waiter on the faculty table. One of the benefits was we got to eat what was left over from their dinner: steak, fish, roast beef—which made it worthwhile putting up with the faculty eating habits. We also were able to take a box of fruit with us after we were done. Ruf North, who was one of our top resident comedians, asked me to remember him with a box of fruit, which I did. As he opened it in his room, a number of fruit flies flew out of the box, and I never heard the end of it. He dumped the fruit and had joke material for the next week.

Moe and the Rule Book

My good friend Patrick Joseph Mulvehill was in and out of the seminary a few times. When he returned to the major seminary, the dean of the building had his two names mixed up, so he called him Joseph instead of Patrick. Moe never corrected him, so he was called Joseph until he was kicked out. I call him Joseph the Simple for the fun of it, even to this day.

One evening, Moe was sitting in the toilet and wrote the entire rule book for the seminary on a roll of toilet paper. He then sent it to Archbishop William O. Brady with the note, "This is what I think of your seminary rules."

He was called in by the rector Big Lou McCarthy and was expelled on the spot. Moe and I still keep in touch and frequently socialize together with our wives.

We Need Real Men in the Priesthood

After being in the major seminary a couple of years, I thought it may be better if I joined the army and spent two years there and then come back if I still felt like becoming a priest. One of the local parish priests heard about my thinking and came to see me. He pounded me on the chest and said, "We need real men in the priesthood."

Looking around the seminary, I tended to agree with him. He said if I became a priest, I could be a chaplain in the military if it was important for me to serve my country. He had been a chaplain himself. He was ahead of his time and instituted a number of progressive ideas in his parish, which was a neighbor to my home parish in Richfield. He would end up preaching at my first Mass. He became an alcoholic and was dismissed from ministry for inappropriately touching a student while he was a chaplain at St. Thomas University. He was a homosexual who acted out rather than controlling his interests in other men.

Tonsure and a Close Call

The process of becoming a priest requires the candidate to go through a series of religious commitments. It starts with tonsure followed by subdeaconite, deaconite, and then the priesthood itself. At each step, one must be approved by the seminary faculty.

Tonsure means "to shear." It started in the Catholic Church at the end of the fifth century, so it is not in the Bible. The bishop actually cuts a little lock of hair from the candidate's head as a sign of commitment to the clerical life. One often sees pictures of monks with a circle of their hair cut down to the bare head.

As I walked down the hallway one evening after brushing my teeth and washing up, I was met by our dean of Grace Hall, Father Patrick Ahern. He now taught history to us after one of the ancient professors finally retired. Father Ahern once said he wished he was back in the seminary like us again. We all groaned and laughed and said, "Sure," in unison.

He said, "You know why?"

"Why?" we said again in unison

"So I could quit."

We really laughed then. But I think he meant it.

As I passed him in the hallway that one night, I think I could smell alcohol on him. It was after nine, and he must have been out for dinner and drinks with friends.

He said, "Christian, are you going to goose someone with that toothbrush?"

I took the brush out of my mouth and laughed.

He then said, "They wanted to clip you at the last faculty meeting, but I told them we need some priests with some spirit, and they passed on you for tonsure."

I figured Father Jerome D. Quinn (JDQ), the scripture teacher, recommended I be clipped. I always had my own interpretation on scripture, and he didn't like it. He gave me a D in scripture. It was the only D I would receive in my schooling, even up to my PhD from Michigan State. I figured Father Jim Moudry, the moral theologian, brother of Monsignor Dick Moudry, and Father Ahern voted for me, and Big Lou McCarthy thought he couldn't kick out another Christian brother.

I breathed heavy and received tonsure, but I came mighty close to being gone again.

Another Black Student Leaves Mysteriously

We had two black seminarians while I was in school. They used to tell the joke about the young black boy walking by a Catholic Church in the Deep South, and an older man made the sign of the cross as he passed by the church. The black boy following a little behind him did the same. The pastor of the church saw what was happening, and he came down the steps of the church and caught up to the black boy and said, "Son, are you a Catholic?"

The black boy said, "No. It's tough enough just being black in the South, much less also being a Catholic."

One of our black seminarians had been a marine and was from out of state. He was put on the carpet once in dogma class and had to try to answer a number of questions on the past and present lessons. He had all kinds of problems trying to struggle through the experience. We called it being in the "barrow." I guess it was considered a test to see how you could think on your feet and react to being challenged. He did not do well.

I thought it was unfair to humiliate him, but I kept my mouth shut. Shortly after that, the student left the seminary. I was having a hard time with the way he was treated, so I thought about going into the rector and telling him the situation and that we needed black vocations. I mentioned my idea to a couple of my classmates, and one pulled me aside and said that this person had been dismissed because he made sexual advances toward another student. That stopped me in my tracks. I knew how something like that came down. As I thought back, I remember that person walking around before lights out with his bathrobe on with a cup of hot chocolate in his hand. He had a quiet, gentle personality and laughed easily, but he was acting out his homosexual feelings, and that meant celibacy could be a problem for him. I put my head down and went on with seminary life.

Subdeacon

One of the major orders on the way to the priesthood is becoming a subdeacon. It started in AD 255 under Pope Cornelius. A subdeacon can prepare the altar for Mass, handle the chalice and bread, read the epistles, and—here is the breaker—agree to celibacy. We were told that a priest has to be totally dedicated to God. No wife or children can get in the way. I often thought that a married person can also be totally dedicated to God by loving his or her spouse and children and loving his or her neighbor as himself or herself. It could include their work, volunteer efforts, and just being as good a person as they could be. But we were brainwashed into thinking celibacy was a necessary component to being a priest. It was a sacrifice one needed to serve God and people better. Later, I would see married Protestant ministers, rabbis, and Eastern rite religious doing the same thing I was doing and often times better than we priests.

I still remember a classmate of my brother Ed, Hank Christensen, say, "Stop and think. You will never have children or grandchildren as a father or grandfather."

I plan to go into more detail on this idea later on in this book when I decide to resign the priesthood.

The Diaconite

The final step before one becomes a priest is the diaconate. The diaconate is mentioned twenty-nine times in the New Testament. It includes both women and men as deacons and deaconesses. Deacons can perform marriages, conduct funerals, baptize, give homilies, and give out communion. I remember a priest saying when the Roman Catholic Church revived the deaconate for married people that it would set back the possibility of priests ever being able to marry for generations. Technically, deacons can go out to parishes and help out. In our day as seminarians, we really did not go to parishes until we were actually ordained. Today deacons as seminarians do go out, and many parishes have married laymen as deacons. I believe the Catholic Church does not want to have women become deaconesses because it is one step from being ordained as priests. It is one of the recommendations I will have in my letter to Pope Francis in chapter 7.

Chapter 4

Ordination to the Priesthood

We were in the final stages of preparing for the priesthood. Even though I was in the seminary for twelve years, I had the scary feeling I was not prepared enough. We were steeped in the classics and philosophy and theology, but not in how to work with women, men, and children and their problems. What about marriage preparation (even though we had a course on marriage), general counseling, convert classes? I shook it off by saying to myself that I would just have to use my common sense when I was sent out into the real world and have to perform my daily responsibilities. What I didn't know myself, I would have to look for resources and make referrals such as sending people to a marriage counselor if they were having marital problems.

The final step to ordination was learning to say Mass. We went to Mass every day, but being the cel-

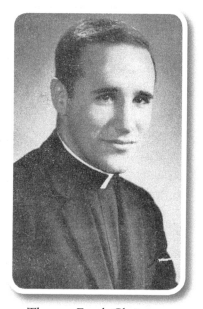

Thomas Frank Christian was ordained as a Roman Catholic priest on February 2, 1963. He served the people in Roseville, Hopkins and Glen Lake/Minnetonka, Minnesota. He took a special interest in helping individuals in trouble with the law in detention facilities, courts, and correctional institutions.

ebrant was a different matter. That meant learning by heart the opening Latin prayers and all the responses to the Latin prayers. Although I knew the altar server's words for years, we said them fast and did not translate them in our minds. I did not know the priest's parts by heart, and we had to memorize them. I studied them and then went in for the final test. I struggled through because I was now alone and not in the congregation where you could hear everybody else and go with the flow. The priest who gave me the test was one of the good guys, Father James Moudry, the new moral theology teacher. It was his brother, Father Dick Moudry, who had helped me through the sex-attack attempt years before. Father Moudry told me to study a little more and come back. I did and had no more trouble. By the way, Jim Moudry resigned a few years later and got married.

Later, as I first said Mass, I had to work at remembering all the exact Latin words at the beginning. A year after I was ordained, the Mass was said in English. The Vatican Council thought it was better for everybody if they could understand what they were saying. My Latin training now would come in handy, as I said, for the television show *Jeopardy* and crossword puzzles.

February 2, 1963, was the day for our ordination. We were all at the great St. Paul Cathedral, and our family and friends were there. Archbishop Byrne started the prayers, and we were underway. Part of the ceremony had us lie on the cold marble floor. Lying there, I kept saying, "I can do this. Now I will be able to save the world."

It was all a daze as the choir sang and the ceremony carried on. The older priests then came up and gave us their blessing by placing their hand on our head. After it was all over, we met with family and friends, and I thought when people get married, they too are on cloud nine and don't remember all the details.

My First Mass

The next day, I had my own first Mass at my home parish at St. Peter's in Richfield. Father William Brand was our master of ceremonies. He was one of my inspirations growing up. He had been made a monsignor and was dressed in all his red robes. But he had a problem with alcohol now and was under the influence that day. He did fine and seemed proud that one of his disciples had made good.

Tom's first mass was at his home parish, St. Peter's Church in Richfield, Minnesota. This is the Christian family. Seated are his father, Edward, and his mother, Ruth. Behind are (left to right) Mike, Dave, Tom, Ed, and Ken.

I asked Father Al Longley to preach, and he also did a great job. However, he too was alcoholic and would be released later from the active priesthood for soliciting a male student at St. Thomas University. I knew he was gay and alcoholic, but he was a leader in the liturgical movement, and I didn't know he was active in his sexual preference.

I would learn that a number of priests were alcoholic, medicating their loneliness with alcohol.

The Knights of Columbus marched in ahead of me and, after Mass, led the procession out. I thanked them for their support, and later, I would join and become a fourth-degree knight myself.

The parish had a beautiful reception for me and my family. My father always said I would get a good education, but I don't know if he thought I would ever make it all the way and become a priest. My mother was a convert from Lutheranism, so she was proud of me and would become more involved in the Catholic Church with a group called the Legion of Mary in our home parish at St. Peter's in Richfield. My brothers Ken and Ed were there. Both of them had been kicked out of the seminary, so they had a very good idea what I had gone through to finally get to be ordained. My two younger brothers Dave and Mike had their own lives and went to the nearest Catholic high school, DeLaSalle, in Minneapolis. I would find out later what they really thought.

I had small prayer cards made up with my picture and information on one side and Jesus, the Good Shepherd, on the other. I had a black enamel chalice with gold interior made in Switzerland. A gold cross was on the stem. One of my nicknames was "Blackie," so the chalice fit my resume. I quoted the Song of Songs 1:6: "I am black and beautiful" (New Revised Standard Version). The explanation was on a table with the chalice. It stated that I was brought up in Richfield, and our farm had rich black dirt to show my solid foundation. My hands were black from picking potatoes from the ground, but I never felt they were dirty. The original words are of a woman expressing her love for her husband. She was dark from working in the vineyards for her family. For the Jews, it was an expression of love between God and his chosen people. Christians saw it as love between Christ and his church. It also reminded people that the chalice was the cup of salvation, and over half of God's people were black. I would tell people we were all one human family and gathered for Mass to give thanks and break bread together to receive the message of the Bible and Holy Communion, the bread of life and the cup of salvation, so we could be strengthened to live our daily lives as Christians.

Before I had the chalice consecrated, I brought it home to my own family, and we all drank from it at our dinner meal. My brother Ken and his wife, Ellen, had their little daughter Lisa Marie take the cup when it was her turn to drink, and she bit into the gold rim. Her tooth mark is there today. When I would talk to children about the fact we were all sisters and brothers in God's family and we ate the bread of life and drank the cup of salvation, they smiled and said they just wanted to see Lisa's tooth mark on the rim of the cup.

I would preach on the black cup once each year when I was a priest. People even now talk about the black cup when we reminisce. We still use it for religious family events. Father Ray Monsour used it for years when he said Spanish Mass for migrant workers.

Assignments

After we were ordained, we had four months before we were given our marching orders to a given parish or other assignment. Each weekend, we were sent to one of the parish churches in the Archdiocese of St. Paul and Minneapolis. We now could drive our own car and come back to the seminary parking lot. My first assignment was to St. John's Parish in New Brighton, Minnesota. The pastor was old school. One of my first duties was to hear children's confessions. The Catholic school was from first to eight grades. This meant after the first and second graders had received their first confession and Holy Communion, they were ready for weekly confession. The nuns and lay teachers would march them into church, and hundreds would line up for confession.

We later would say it was like getting stoned to death by popcorn.

As I started to hear my first children's confessions, I told them we were all sisters and brothers in God's human family, and we should learn from our parents and teachers and have fun playing with our classmates. I gave them one Our Father to say as a penance to remind us that God is our Father and loves us.

It didn't take long before the pastor knocked on my confessional and told me I had to hurry up and not take so long with each child. I cut my words of wisdom down considerably, but within minutes, the good father knocked on the confessional door again and told me to get moving faster. After a couple more warnings, I told each child that God loves us, and we are all sisters and brothers—period.

I thought there must be a better way to hear confessions, and finally, in my third parish, we tried communal confession, absolving each person as they came up the aisle after thinking as a group about their individual responsibilities and singing together and saying a communal penance. We got called into the archbishop's office and told we could only do that if the ship was sinking or the plane was going to crash. Too bad, because it made a lot more sense. We had people come up after our communal confession with tears in their eyes because they felt so much better.

My First Assignment

St. Rose of Lima, Roseville, Minnesota

After our weekly duties, we finally received our marching orders to go full-time to a parish in June of 1963.

Roseville is a suburb of St. Paul, and the pastor was a little Irishman named Monsignor Jimmy. He was made a monsignor for his past work in the archdiocese. I replaced Father Tom Garvey, who moved up the ladder. He was a good man and did most of the work for the monsignor. The second assistant now became the first assistant. His name was Father Roger Hessian. Roger and I were in the seminary together. He was two years ahead of me, and at one time, while we were in high school, he was the prefect over me my sophomore year. He knew that I was a troublemaker and had a hard time keeping me from goofing off. Because the seminary was so confining, a number of us looked for opportunities to let off steam. Roger never held it against me because I think he knew that the seminary was not a natural environment. He got the nickname "Hoot" after Hoot Gibson, a sidekick of Randolph Scott, a Western movie star. In the seminary, on some Saturday evenings, Father Karl would bring in an old harmless Randolph Scott movie. Now Hoot and I were on the same side, saving all the people in Roseville, Minnesota.

I was assigned to St. Rose for two years and thoroughly enjoyed it. We had an elementary school from first to eighth grade, run by the Servite Sisters of Ladysmith, Wisconsin, and six lay teachers.

My first introduction to the nuns came from the principal Sister Rosalie Hennessey. She was very attractive and outgoing, and she knew how to manipulate people, especially men. She announced at our first meeting in the convent next door to the school that as the second assistant, I would have to take two nuns to the store each week to buy groceries. I answered that I would rather teach the nuns how to drive and that, as adults, they could get their own groceries. They all laughed, but I never heard another word about driving them to the store again.

Hoot and I would teach in the school, visit the local nursing homes, run the youth group, conduct adult instruction classes, prepare couples for their wedding, baptize babies, and adult converts. I took a special interest in criminal justice resources. I counseled at Woodview Juvenile Detention Center, and I was on the Ramsey County Traffic Court Education Panel and visited people in the local county jail.

We were busy and had one day off, Mondays. I would normally say six-thirty Mass and then go home to see my family and then visit friends. Being a little overzealous, I would stop and teach a class on religion at Our Lady of Peace, a high school for girls from eight to nine. A classmate of ours, Harry "the Horse" Reilly's sister was a nun teaching there, so I volunteered to help her out one day a week. At age twenty-five, I never thought about burning out.

Hoot and I had events for the teenagers, and in those days, hootenannies were big (not named after Hoot Hessian). They were like a dance-and-song fest, and the kids loved them. Cyril Paul, my classmate from St. John's University, had a calypso group, and we paid them a hundred dollars to headline the evening.

Cyril also sang at a local bar called the Flame Room, and they would have limbo contests. I would often join friends at the end of my day off and have a beer with them. Of course, I had to enter the limbo contests, and because I was a catcher in baseball, I could go low and win the contests even with a brace on my left knee from my old football injury.

My old friend Patrick Joseph Mulvehill was now married, and I would stop by and see him and his wife, La Vonne. One evening, as I was walking down their steps to go home, Pat had the bright idea to flip for fifty-cent pieces. I lost thirteen in a row, and we finally flipped double or nothing, and I finally won. Pat was always good to get a poker game going on my Mondays off. One time, we played into the wee hours of the morning. I finally got home about 4:00 a.m. As I quietly walked down the hall of the rectory to my bedroom, the phone rang. It was the nursing home. One of the old-timers was getting ready to go to the happy hunting grounds, and they needed a priest. I had not even started to take off my clothes for bed, so I jumped into the car and was there in a New York minute. The nurses were amazed at my speed and freshness to anoint the man for his last journey. I was up two hours later to say six-thirty Mass and start a new day. I have to admit that like the monks at St. John's Abbey, getting up at four o'clock twice a day was part of my secret.

The Banana Boat

One of the teachers named Bill was the athletic director hired by Monsignor Jimmy to work with the kids at physical education and after-school games. I knew his brother George from the seminary, so we became instant friends. He ran a stock car at the local racetracks, and I would go see him once in a while. My cousin Don Haeg was the Minnesota stock-car champion, and when we were younger, we would go see him race. Bill let me run a warm-up race one time. I could barely see with all the mud and open windshield, so I knew I was not cut out to be a threat for the Indianapolis 500.

One day, Bill and I were talking, and he said he was taking a vacation after Easter to the Bahamas Islands. He asked if I could use my vacation time to join him. I checked with the Monsignor and Hoot and got approval. After Easter, things slowed down; and if I could leave Monday and be back by Friday, everything would be golden.

On the plane, Bill told me he had a ring and was going to ask one of the nurses volunteering one year in the Bahamas to become engaged to him. I had met the girl because her sister taught first grade. She had come last year to talk to her sister's class dressed in her nurse's uniform and nurse's hat. I was impressed, and so were the kids. I told Bill to go for it.

As we got off the plane, I had my cowboy boots on and my cowboy hat. I was ready to party. We met all the volunteers and went out with them the first night to a local bar called the Banana Boat. Everyone was dancing and having a good time. I asked one of the Bahamian ladies to dance, but she turned me down. As I was watching our group, someone came up and took one of our chairs. The place was packed, so I told the native Bahamian that that chair was taken, and our group was out dancing. He looked at me, as if to say, *So what, man?* I followed him over to where he sat down on our chair. I again told him that chair was already taken, and he gave me another one of his looks. As I walked away, I turned and grabbed the chair with two hands and pulled it away from him. He hit the floor with a thud. As I walked back to our table with our chair, I knew he was coming. He said something about my mother, so I was more than ready for him. I set the chair down at our table and turned to greet him. I had my back to the wall, so no one could sucker punch me. Having boxed and wrestled, I thought, *Here we go again. I will have to seek justice for him illegally taking the chair and, of course, defend myself … right?* He took a swing at me, and I weaved to the right and straightened him up with a left jab and dropped him with a right cross. He went down like a ton of bricks.

To my surprise, the whole place went up for grabs. People were hitting one another left and right. Beer bottles were being busted over people's heads. I just stood my ground, and if anybody got into my face, I let them know not to come back. The bouncers were there, and I said, "I am cool and ready to leave." Like the Richard Prior movie again. We backed out to the car, which was a little Volkswagen. The chair thief was up now and stood behind the bouncers and using the f-word like a comma. Someone said I was a priest. Our chair-thief friend said he didn't care if I was a "fucking priest." I took offence at that and went around the bouncers and said, "What did you say?" He repeated it, but when he got to the *f* part, I dropped him one more time. We quickly got into the car and drove as fast as we could. Beer cans and glass bottles were flying at the car. The word was that one of the bouncers had a gun and had his hand on it and was close to using it. Today he may have used it.

The next day, we were relaxing on the beach when one of the volunteer missionary priests, John Prinzing, came by to say hello. I had gone to St. John's University with him, and he was now serving in the Bahamas. He said some guy with cowboy boots and a cowboy hat tore up the Banana Boat last night. As I had my cowboy hat tipped down on my face to protect me from the sun, I raised it up to talk to him. He said, "It was you, wasn't it?"

As we were flying back that Friday, I asked Bill if he ever gave his girlfriend the ring. He said, "No, the opportunity never presented itself."

The Banana Boat story follows me wherever I go. There were people who were in the Bahamas at the time who heard about it, and they continue to tell the story. It just happened again fifty years later. My niece and her husband were talking to Tom Diffly, their realtor, who had been there; and when he found out they were related to me, the story came up again in glorious color. However, my pastor Monsignor Jimmy never heard about it, and neither was it reported to the archbishop. Bill's girlfriend didn't talk to me when she got back from her volunteer work. Things would eventually, however, change for the better.

Hoot Hessian and I continued to work each day until Christmas 1964. Monsignor Jimmy and his cousin Agatha, his old housekeeper, still lived in the parish house with us. She would go with him every-where as if they were a married couple. I am positive they just had a good relationship. It did make celibacy a little more livable.

They always took six weeks off and went to Florida after Christmas. This year was no exception. However, one of the nuns who taught seventh grade decided to leave the convent. Sister Rosalie, the principal, because Monsignor Jimmy had already left for vacation, turned to me and said, "What are we going to do? School starts January 2, and we have no replacement for her."

I calmly said we put an ad in the paper for a seventh grade teacher. We received four applicants. One stood out with a college degree from St. John's University and a master's degree from St. Thomas University and four years of experience teaching grade school at Assumption Grade School in Richfield. We interviewed all four, and the top candidate with all those credentials happened to be Cyril Paul, my classmate, and the one who sang at our youth group hootenannies. He also was black. This was a suburban parish, and there were no black families in the area.

"What will the monsignor say?" Sister Rosalie sighed.

I told her you send him a telegram and tell him the nun had left, and you conducted interviews with four candidates, and Cyril was heads and shoulders above the rest. The monsignor telegrammed back that under no circumstances could she hire Cyril Paul because he was too controversial.

"Now, what?" Sister Rosalie said.

January 2 was a couple of days away. It was too late. I told her to telegram the monsignor that school was starting, and she already offered the job to Cyril.

Cyril Paul became the seventh grade teacher, and the kids loved him. Now they wanted to go to Mass because he led them in song, and Hoot and I made the Mass fit our audience. We talked about the Bible teaching us how to enjoy life, and Holy Communion is our family meal giving us strength to be better girls and boys. Cyril was a teacher in Trinidad and a police officer in the Bahamas before he came to Minnesota on a scholarship. He talked the queen's English and had all kinds of interesting examples to bring to the classroom.

In June of 1965, the lay teachers renewed their contracts. Monsignor notified Sister Rosalie that he would not approve Cyril Paul's contract for the next year. He had gotten pressure from some of the parents of the seventh graders. They were not comfortable with a black man teaching their daughters. When push came to shove, the monsignor gave two examples: One, Cyril Paul used the word *asi-*

nine in the classroom. His other concern was that, as Mr. Paul was walking up the aisle in the classroom, he noticed one of the girls had dropped something. He picked it up and handed it to her and said, "Is this yours?"

It was her purse, and a sanitary napkin had fallen out.

Sister Rosalie and her staff were very upset when it looked like Cyril would not be with them in the fall.

"What can we do now?" they said.

I asked them if they felt there was just cause for not renewing Cyril Paul's contract. To a person, they said, "No!"

I told Sister Rosalie the Servite Sisters could tell the monsignor they would not teach at St. Rose of Lima School if Cyril's contract was not renewed. She said they could not go that far. They needed the school for vocations to the Servite Order. They had a number of girls over the years enter their order after eighth grade.

I said, then how about the lay teachers sending a letter to the monsignor, signed by all of them, that they would not accept a contract unless Cyril Paul received one. They all agreed.

Cyril's contract was renewed. He taught for four more years and then went into one of the larger companies in Minneapolis as a diversity counselor.

That, however, was not the end of this story. After Cyril received his contract, I got a letter from the archbishop saying that I was transferred to the other side of the Twin Cities; namely, Hopkins, a suburb on the west side of Minneapolis.

Before I left, the monsignor called me into his room and asked me to do him one favor: "Take Cyril Paul with you."

I told him I could get a job anywhere in the archdiocese, but Cyril Paul could not.

I liked the old monsignor. He was of the old school. He always treated me right. He told me to keep up the good work on my sermons when he received a compliment on my homilies from parishioners.

I had one other disagreement with the monsignor. Earlier, my brother Dave was in the military, and there was a spinal meningitis epidemic at Fort Sill, Oklahoma. Dave was struck, and the two soldiers on either side of him died. He was breathing shallow and looked like he might not make it. My parents were called to come to the hospital. I told them I would get permission to go with them. The monsignor told me the parish duties could not get along without me, and I could not go. I told my parents to go and let me know how Dave was doing. If he was not going to make it, I would tell the monsignor that my priorities were family first, and I was leaving to be with my brother and my parents. My parents called when they got there, and Dave had taken a turn for the better, and he was going to make it. Dave served his two years in the army and got married to Irma Frenning, and they had a girl they named Michelle. Pneumococcal meningitis broke loose from his chest when he had the flu thirteen years later and entered his sinuses and then his brain. He died at age thirty-six, but if they would have given him the proper medicine like penicillin, he may have recovered.

As I was leaving St. Rose, I told the monsignor that I had fourteen days of vacation coming, and I had written to Omaha and gotten Father Donald to come and take my place. I would have to cancel him coming. The monsignor told me he was so upset about the Cyril Paul episode that he would take the vacation himself and not to cancel it.

After I got to St. John's parish in Hopkins, I received a call from Sister Rosalie. She said, "There is a God!"

Father Donald had come to St. Rose in his clerical suit and Roman collar and rang the doorbell of the rectory. Agatha came to the door and saw he was black, which I did not know at the time. She closed the door and left him standing on the steps and ran down the hall to get the monsignor. Monsignor opened the door and explained that Father Christian had been transferred, and his own services were no longer needed. Father Donald said he would be going to the University of Minnesota for a special class he had signed up for, and at the moment, he had no other place to go. Monsignor Jimmy let him in, and he stayed the two weeks and said Mass for the people daily and on Sundays and visited a number of families in the parish. The monsignor took the two weeks of vacation.

The following Christmas, the monsignor and his cousin Agatha prepared to leave for six weeks after New Year's.

Hoot Hessian had different ideas. He had stood by helpless as I was transferred to the other side of town. It was his turn now to act. He wrote the monsignor a letter and left it at his office. Hoot informed him that this year, he would take the six weeks of vacation and would see them when he got back. When he returned in mid-February, he was informed that he too was moved to a faraway parish. This was Hoot's passive-aggressive way of showing his displeasure with the Cyril Paul debunker and his support for me.

I went to a meeting in St. Louis a couple of years later, and a black priest came up to me and said, "Are you Tom Christian?" I said I was, and he said, "You son of a bitch, I am Father Donald." We both had a good laugh as he told me his version of the story.

At our fiftieth St. John's University class reunion in 2009, people stood up and told stories about our time at St. John's. Cyril Paul, who was now famous for all the things he had done for the monks and St. John's University, thanked me publicly for what I had done for him in hiring him back at St. Rose of Lima School in 1965. I was touched by his words.

My Second Assignment

St. John the Evangelist Parish
Hopkins and Interlachen Park, Minnesota

My new pastor was Father Leo Howley. He told me that he heard I had vacation coming, and in June, things were slow, so I should take two weeks off and enjoy myself. That was a great way to start a new assignment.

Father Howley had a hard laugh and seemed to be happy to have help again. He told me that when he was a young priest, he had to say the six-thirty Mass each morning, so that would be what I would have to do. That was okay with me. A good thing he said was that, on Sundays, we would take turns preaching. That meant we only had to prepare one sermon every two weeks.

My first sermon was on my black chalice. I had given it once a year at St. Rose and "with the kids at school," so I had that one down. After I preached that Sunday, Father Howley said, "So now we have a real preacher!"

The next Sunday, Father Howley preached a scripture lesson better than we had in the seminary. He prided himself on his knowledge of the Bible. He had to outdo me, and he did.

He also told me that when he was first assigned his own parish out in the country, he was so lonely that he tried drinking alcohol to drown his sorrows. He said he got sick rather than become an alcoholic like some of his classmates.

Father Howley told me I was in charge of the youth group. I told him I would be happy to work with the youth, but I wanted to serve all the people in a number of ways.

Father Howley took all the baptisms, weddings, and funerals. I was left with everything when he was on his vacation. Now, there are normally stipends for all the extra personal ceremonies, but he told me later this was a one-collection parish. People gave in one envelope on Sunday, and that was it—no nickel-and-dime situation for the people of Interlachen Park. Part of the parish was a very well-to-do area, and it made sense.

George Mikan, the great Minneapolis and Los Angeles Lakers basketball player, was in our parish. I remember shaking hands with him and looking up to him at six feet ten inches. My hand was like a child's hand in his.

I still remember when I was in grade school back at St. Peter's, and our basketball team played at the Lakers halftime game. I did not remind George Mikan that I used to shoot free throws like him, and his swearing when he was elbowed on his hook shoot scandalized our young minds. He was still our hero.

Father Howley, with his forced laugh, soon became known by me to my friends and classmates as "Happy" Howley. It didn't take long for "Happy" to become unhappy. He had me attend his daily 8:00 a.m. Mass. In those days, laypeople were not reading the epistles or serving as Eucharistic ministers, so that was my job. For the prayers of the faithful, I had to sing them. It was no problem except, one day, Happy preached on St. Eusibius. He was an Italian saint who was not accepted by the local people. Happy compared himself to St. Eusibius. As pastor, he said many people did not agree with him; and just as St. Eusibius was persecuted, so as pastor, he too was persecuted for his leadership. When it came time to sing the Prayers of the Faithful, I proclaimed, "We pray for our holy father Pope John, our archbishop Leo Binz, and our persecuted pastor Father Leo. We pray to the Lord." The people responded, "Lord, hear our prayer." There were maybe forty people attending Mass that morning, and they all doubled up laughing.

Happy just about fell off his presiding throne (the chair was at the middle and behind the altar that faced the people). He went on with the Mass and never said a word to me.

A few weeks later, we had one of our parishioners go through a heart bypass surgery. This was 1966, and they were not as common as today. I went to visit him, and he was all hooked up to machines and in a coma. He was a young family man in his early forties and looked as strong as an ox. If anybody could make it, he could.

At Mass the next day, I again sang the Prayers of the Faithful. This time, along with the normal prayers, I included one for him. I sang, "We pray for our brother (his name) that he may heal and come back to our community and make his contribution."

It didn't come out right. It sounded like we were waiting for him to come back and put his envelope in the collection basket. Happy struck. He said it was embarrassing, and I could no longer sing or say the Prayers of the Faithful.

Because Happy wanted me to stick to the youth group and stay away from adult parishioners, I got the young people together, and we decided to have a variety show. Kids could play their instruments, sing solo or in a group, and some did skits. It was like hootenanny time again. I got Cyril Paul and the Monarchs to be the lead act. The kids emceed and were all into it. They made signs and posters and put them up all over town. There would be an entrance fee of one dollar, which would pay Cyril and his people one hundred dollars, and the rest would go to the youth group for dances, ski trips, and other activities.

Happy struck again. The afternoon, before the evening performance, he announced to me that there could not be a fee. We were
a one-envelope parish, and we could not "nickel and dime" people.
Did I forget?

No problem. There was no charge. The kids put a banner across
all the signs that it was now a free show.

The place was packed. The kids had a ball, and Cyril was better than ever. I gave Cyril a hundred dollars from my pocket. It was
worth it. Happy was not happy with the great turnout. I, of course,
did not tell him I had covered the expense. He thought he won.

Parents came up after the show and said this was the best thing
that ever happened to their parish. Entire families were able to attend
together. They were proud of their teenagers and the community
feeling it generated.

Two men asked me how we could afford the costs without a
fee. I said it was covered by a silent donor. They asked Cyril his fee,
and he said he was paid the standard one hundred dollars, and he
was happy. Later that evening, the two men came up to me during
refreshments and handed me an envelope. "This is to add to the
silent-donor money," they said. There was a hundred dollars in cash
in the envelope. I won, and Happy didn't even know about it. His
spies were in the dark too.

Each Sunday that Happy preached, he had his scripture down
pat. People told me that they never heard him so good.

One week, I received a postcard unsigned. It said next Sunday
was my turn to preach. "Do us a favor and prepare something." I
took it to Happy and told him I had some fan mail. He said he didn't
know anything about it, but maybe I should take it to heart. That
Sunday, I brought the card to the pulpit. Because it was not signed, I
said it was hard to respond. I told the people I read the scripture for
the Sunday, and I tried to look in the paper and talk to people about
how we could apply the readings to our daily life. I told them if they
told me how it could apply more to their lives, I could improve my
sermons too. If I could go back to my preparation, I think I should
have spent more time on making my sermons relevant. The postcard
writer, whoever she or he was, was right. Happy did have a woman

who did a lot of work around the parish and was a very intelligent person. If I had to bet, I think she was the ghost writer and one of his spies.

I think I did get her back one time. I had baptisms when Happy was on vacation. Days after the baptism, the mother asked to take instructions to become a Catholic. Her husband was Catholic, and now that their baby was baptized, she felt she should become Catholic too. She said she was impressed with the way I had of explaining the baptismal ceremony and including the welcome to our worshiping community of their little baby.

After a series of instructions, it became obvious that she liked talking to me more than learning about salvation history and becoming Catholic. Her husband traveled a lot. I turned to Happy's helper and told her I was just about finished with the convert lessons—and because the young lady was very attractive and getting too friendly, I was getting uncomfortable—would she finish the lessons and welcome her to the Catholic faith woman to woman? She did. The couple eventually got divorced.

One time, Happy was on the phone talking to a priest friend. Because Happy talked and laughed loud, I often could hear him from my room down the hall. This time, he was telling his listener that Father Mark Farrell from New Prague, a parish south of the cities, told him, "Give me Christian, and I will break him." At the time, I thought, *Bring him on.* In the seminary, they could kick you out. It is a little harder once you are ordained, as we would find out with cases of pedophile priests. I will go into detail about them later in our story.

I did have the habit of giving the archbishops Byrnes and Binz ammunition. I had a couple come in one day. He had been married before, and according to the rules, she could not get married in the Catholic Church because he was a baptized Christian. I thought that was poor. Today it looks like Pope Francis agrees with me. I told her we could not perform the ceremony in the Catholic Church, but after they got married by a judge or whomever, they should come back to see me, and I would give them a blessing if it would help them in their marital relationship. She did, and I did. I told her that she should not tell people but be at ease with her new marriage. Of course, her new husband told his ex-wife, who told the local Catholic pastor, who called me. Fortunately, the pastor was Father Tony Lewis, who was a friend of mine. He told me I could get in trouble if the chancery heard about it. I never told Happy, and I would do it again and again.

Another time, a young woman came in to talk to me. She said she had been in the military and had been raped. She now considered herself a lesbian. I talked to her about how terrible her situation in the military was, and she should report it to the authorities, including the police. She said she tried, but it went nowhere. Those problems continue to exist as we know even today. But now it is more in the open and is being addressed by political pressure.

I talked to her about getting professional counseling to work out her feelings. To give up on men was understandable, but given time, she may meet someone whom she could spend the rest of her life with and be happy, and it could be a man or a woman. She said she did, and it was a woman. We were not trained in same sex relationships, and the Catholic Church was against them. I told her this, but I also said that a true relationship between people who loved each other cannot be bad. I told her to take her time and work out her feelings with an understanding counselor who was not Catholic. Today I would have told her not to worry about same sex relationships. The fact that she had been raped and that caused her to go for a same sex partner was the reason I told her to take her time and work out her feelings. She said she did not have these feelings toward men until she had been raped.

That evening, Happy asked me about the young woman who came in for counseling. I told him it was private and confidential. He blew his top. He was the pastor and needed to know everything that was going on in his domain. He sputtered and hemmed and hawed, but I just let him stew.

On my time off, I continued to play softball and touch football. One time on a Saturday morning, I was playing in a softball tournament, and we were winning. The sacrament of penance was always scheduled for 4:30 p.m. and again at 7:30 p.m. The semifinal game was at 3:00 p.m. I called Happy and told him the problem. If he could take the 4:30 p.m. time, I would take all of the 7:30 p.m. time.

He always called me "father" even though we were generations apart. His answer to my request was, "Father, your responsibilities are here," and he would not bend. I told him fine, and I would be there. As I heard confessions, it seemed there were more than normal. I had the sneaking feeling that once I started, he left me to take all the people who came that afternoon. He may have even called some of his spies to come in to make it a full-time job. That evening, there were few confessions. Happy won that one.

I have to admit that being with Happy was not too bad. He tried to bully me and to outdo me, but I did not see us in competition. But I guess he did.

Our Father, Edward Howard Christian, Dies

On February 15, 1966, our father suffered a cerebral hemorrhage. He had gotten up at 7:00 a.m. to get ready to go on the eight-to-four shift for the Richfield Police Department. He went into the bathroom to shower and shave and went down. My mother heard him fall and ran to see what was the matter. She couldn't open the bathroom door because he had it blocked by his body. She called the police department. One of their own was down. The ambulance rushed him to Saint Mary's Hospital in downtown Minneapolis. It was 9:00 a.m. when Dr. Jim Arms, our family doctor, told us our dad had suffered a severe cerebral hemorrhage, and he would be gone by 11:00 a.m.

As our family stood at his bedside, I tried to say prayers with them; and at 11:00 a.m., we saw the color leave his face, and he was gone. I still remember our mother's face as she realized at that moment her husband of thirty-five years and father of five boys was leaving us.

He always said when someone passed away that they were going to the happy hunting grounds. Now it was his turn.

He was only sixty-one years old. He was two months from being sixty-two and retired.

One of the nuns, who was there as a nurse, told me now my mother could become my housekeeper because I was a priest. I looked at her and said, "I don't think that is important to me at this time."

I made preparations for our father's funeral with my mother and four brothers. Our home parish was St. Peter's in Richfield. The pastor Father George was on vacation, so his assistant Father Gil was in charge. I told him our family friend Cyril Paul would be the person in charge of the singing. He told me that they had a singer who sang at all the funerals. She was a neighbor of ours, and we had grown up with their children. We knew she was a fine singer and could have been in an opera, but we wanted Cyril Paul, a closer friend and—no offense—a better singer with better songs. Father Gil said he couldn't do that to his pastor Father George. Apparently, Cyril was too liberal with his liturgy. We talked it over with our mother and she said she preferred Cyril too. Our parents had been married in the Assumption Parish, and four generations of our relatives were buried in the Assumption cemetery. We actually had belonged to Assumption and had attended the school there for three years until St. Peter's had been opened in 1945.

We went to Assumption Church, and the Franciscan priest who was the pastor there agreed with us. We told Father Gil that we were moving the funeral. (He later was on the list of priests who were accused of molesting minors, but he turned us down because he did not want to upset his pastor.)

The funeral was the largest ever at the Richfield mortuary. Our dad had lived his whole life in Richfield and farmed and was the second police officer chosen to serve his community. George Brening, our neighbor as we were growing up, was the first. At our father's death, there was a full police force with a chief, Cy Johnson, and a number of officers. Richfield was a suburb of Minneapolis and now needed a full law enforcement team. Our father would be missed and would be tough to replace.

Our father knew almost everybody in the village and used to joke that he took most of his probable arrests home to their families because he knew them, and it would be better to have them think about their behavior rather than have them sit in jail. He had a great sense of humor and was a friend to all. One of his nicknames was "Midnight" because he took his turn on the 12:00 p.m. to 8:00 a.m. shift and would run into many of his friends in the wee hours of the morning.

Another of his nicknames was "Hattie." When at a party, he had the habit of going into the hall closet to hang up his coat on a cold winter evening and come out with one of the funny hats he found. He would put one back and take another, sometimes a women's hat, and walk around the party with that on his head.

At the wake, people of all ages came. He worked the Richfield Mall as one of his beats, which was right across from Holy Angels Academy, so young students came. They didn't say much, and they stood in the back. I made a point to go back and talk to them. One spoke from the group and said, as a police officer, they were always on their guard. But with our dad, because he treated them as individuals and showed them respect, they loved to joke with him. He was their friend.

One young adult told me that he always had time to greet you and talk to you as he walked his beat. She showed me her engagement ring and said she worked at the bakery. All day long, no one noticed her new ring, even her coworkers, even though she flashed it. As Officer Christian came in to say hello, he said, "Congratulations! I see you are engaged." He was the only one who noticed all day.

He proceeded to tell her marriage is as great as the two of you are willing to make it. He said he had been married for thirty-five years and had a great wife and five boys whom he was more than proud of. He said he only had a grade school education, but he told his sons, "Get your education. No one can take that away from you." Of his five sons, two of us would get PhDs, another one a law degree, and another two master's degrees.

An old-timer by the name of Dooley came into the mortuary with two canes and slowly made his way up to the casket. Arthritis was winning the battle. He pulled out his watch, and I heard him say, "Damned if it ain't." I went over to him, and he told me our dad used to stop and see him when he was laid up—one of the few who did. This was the first time he had been out of his house in over twelve months. His daughter drove him over. I asked him about his watch, and he told me it was an old joke that he and my dad had. It involved two bums who had found a pocket watch. Neither could tell time, so when one said to the other, "What time is it?" The other would pull out the watch and show him. The other guy would say, "Damned if it ain't!"

Dooley told me, "When your dad would come to visit me, he we would always take the clock from the dresser and show it to me and say, 'What time is it, Dooley?' and I would say, 'Damned if it ain't.' I had to come to say goodbye and do our watch joke one more time."

The funeral the next day was packed. Cyril Paul led the community in song to celebrate our father's life. Brother Raimond, a Christian brother and another of my classmates who happened to be black, carried the cross as we brought our father's casket down the aisle and into church.

I remembered that as we picked up the garbage for the pigs on the farm at the old soldiers' home, Dad would say, "Hello, Joe Louis," when he saw a black man walking on the grounds. Our father, being from a farm, had only contact with black offenders as a police officer, and here, two black men had prominent roles in his funeral.

I did my best to give the eulogy. I said he was a farmer and worked to help feed his world. He was a peace officer to serve the people in his community. His casket was draped in a white cover to show that he was now on his way to his new life and his own resurrection.

I remember our grandmother Ernestine (Tina) Carney say he never left the house without saying goodbye. I used that at his funeral as we said our last goodbye. I finished my words with, "He was the greatest man I ever knew."

We carried the casket from the church to the cemetery right next door. Jim and Fred Brening, our neighbors who worked at the local Jewish cemetery, had dug the six-foot grave in the Assumption cemetery. Jim told me later it was the hardest hole he ever dug because he knew it was for our dad. On this cold February day in Minnesota, Cyril Paul sang "Deep River." Everyone stood in silence as they listened to the beautiful words on that cold, freezing day.

I told my mother after the funeral I tried to do my best. She smiled and said, "You did."

From that day forward, I would always preach on Father's Day and use some of these ideas. I told people that the concept of God the Father was made real to me when I thought of my own father.

I must say that when I returned to the rectory, Happy Howley was sitting on the porch and available to talk about our father and the funeral. I respected him for that.

My two years at St. John the Evangelist and Happy Houley were drawing to a close. I am sure Happy could have asked the archbishop to keep me for another year or so as his assistant, but there was no doubt that Happy was more than happy to see me move on. My next move was just down the road to Glen Lake/Minnetonka, next to Hopkins and Immaculate Heart of Mary Parish and Father Tony Muscala, pastor.

He would be the greatest guy to work for by far.

My Third Assignment

The Immaculate Heart of Mary Parish

The first contact I had with my new assignment was a few months earlier. Ron Welsch, a priest one year ahead of me in the seminary, had asked me to accompany him as he took the present assistant from Immaculate Heart of Mary (IHM) to a treatment center. Ron was an outspoken liberal priest who made me look like a rookie compared to his ideas. He had an unfortunate experience on his first assignment to be stationed with an alcoholic priest who had a brother who was also a priest and alcoholic, along with a sister who too was alcoholic. Many nights, they would drink together at the parish rectory. The party was always on. Ron had been an A student, and an all-American seminarian. To say he was disillusioned is an understatement. Now he was trying to make the best of it helping others.

We took the assistant from IHM to a program in Wisconsin and met with the intake worker. It was then I found out that the priest was gay and was having major problems being a Catholic priest and being gay. He went through their program and resigned from the priesthood, and I keep in touch with him. He now has a long-term partner and is fine.

Ron Welsh resigned from the priesthood and lost his faith in the Roman Catholic Church. He traveled and eventually married a woman from England and died in his sixties.

As I came to IHM, I found out I was replacing the gay priest. I didn't have a problem with that, and I and the pastor Tony Muscala hit it off right away. He was Polish, and there was a large Polish population in Northeast Minneapolis. In fact, some of the older priests were actually called "Polish princes." Tony was one of them.

Tony was very open and relaxed about almost everything. He too had the arrangement that we would take turns every other Sunday with our preaching. He read his sermon from a book he received each year. I looked at the readings for the coming Sunday and then looked at the paper and radio for what was going on and listened to the people I saw that week and tried to make it relevant to their everyday life. I even had people come to IHM from as far away as Roseville to attend my Mass, but they soon told me it was too hard to travel that far each Sunday. They were disillusioned with their local Mass, and I think they just stopped going to church or only for special occasions.

The parish people at IHM had other alternatives. Some went to the early 7:00 a.m. Mass and got a shortened sermon and were in and out of church in a half an hour. This was for the more conservative people in the parish. The other Masses had a longer sermon and were more attended by most of the parishioners. However, the 10:30 a.m. Mass was a High Mass, and a full choir sang, and a priest from the Franciscan monastery nearby said the Mass. His name was Father Rock Stack and was young and seen as moderate, so if people didn't agree with Father Tony or Father Tom, they went to Father Stack's Mass. We also had a 5:00 p.m. Mass that was attended by the young people. They had their own band, and the sermons were a dialogue. So we tried to have something for everyone.

One Sunday, I went into the pulpit with a large professionally done sign that read, "WHITE RACISM MUST GO." I showed it from side to side so all the people in the church could see it. Then I made a few comments and sat down. I put the sign in my office window at the parish rectory for the rest of my time at IHM. No one threw any rocks at the window. I became very involved in race issues.

At a social party, a woman told me there was no African culture for the Afro-Americans in the United States. I told her that early African culture in Egypt and Africa was ahead of its time. The movie *Roots* showed us how terrible slavery was as Kunta Kinta was kidnaped as he went out looking for material to make his young brother a drum. She only saw the ghetto and the welfare side of the Negro. She did not see slavery as a major cause of the problems we have even today.

In confession, I would hear how the person wanted to sell their house because a black family was moving into his or her block. They didn't want to lose their housing value. It was a tough battle to try to convince them to accept an integrated community.

Our youth group went on ski trips, and I backed teen dances by cosigning a contract with the bands.

One time, Father Ray Monsour and I had a dance for both of our youth groups. He was at St. James Parish in St. Paul, so he brought his group over in a bus. We told our young people to make sure to make both sides feel welcome. It didn't take long, and rumors started flying that there was going to be a fight between the West Seventh tough guys and the suburban gang. I went to our leaders, and Father Ray talked to his people. I told our leader that if a fight broke out, I would search him out, and he would have to fight me. In those days, we could say things like that. He knew I had boxed and wrestled, so he said there would be no trouble, and there wasn't.

At another dance, one kid came up to me and said so and so had a gun. I found the suspect standing near the dance floor, and I put my arm around him and patted him down. He had a starter's pistol in his belt. I pulled it out and said, "What are you going to do with this? Clean your fingernails?" I put it in my belt and told him to see me after the dance. I showed it to a couple of chaperones at cleanup time, and I shot it down the hallway. I often remember the movie star who pointed a starter's pistol at his temple and pulled the trigger. The wad of the bullet killed him. I am glad I didn't aim it at someone as a joke. I respected guns too much, even a starter's pistol.

We had an open confessional room, and people could speak through the traditional screen or come around and sit down on a chair and talk to the priest face-to-face. We actually had two chairs because often husbands and wives and dating couples would venture around the kneeler and screen.

Father Tony and I set up communal confessions, which I described earlier. People came to church, and we would have them sing a song and then think about how they were doing in life. We talked about students, single adults, married people, divorced individuals, parenting, work-related and community responsibilities. Then we had them come up like they did for communion, and we, in the name of Christ, absolved them from all their sins. We then had a community penance, which was one Our Father said together. We ended with another hymn. We announced that if anyone wanted to come back to the confessionals for individual counseling, we were available.

We had people crying they were so happy. This was painless and much more effective. It didn't take long, and Father Tony was called in by the archbishop and told we couldn't do this anymore. General confession is allowed if the ship is sinking. I have been told that some priests have communal penance like we did. Now most people just don't go to confession anymore.

For marriage preparation, we had trained married couples meet with the engaged couples and help them get ready for the big step. Topics included communication, finances, sexuality, parenthood, other relationships like in-laws and friends, and spirituality. Each married couple had their specialty, and Father Tony and I handled the spirituality section.

Glen Lake Home School and Glen Lake TB sanitarium were in our parish boundaries, so we had to take responsibilities to serve the people there. As I had pointed out earlier, I had worked in Roseville at the Woodview Detention facilities, and I had also served on the St. Paul Traffic Court. Monsignor Tom Maugher, the head of Catholic Charites for the St. Paul and Minneapolis Archdiocese, had told me to keep my interest in serving people of all ages in trouble with the law. So I called the present director of Catholic Charities, Father Jerome Boxleitner, and told him I was involved with criminal justice issues before and would be happy to help out at the Hennepin County Glen Lake Home School for delinquent youth. He told me they already had a chaplain by the name of Father Omar from St. John's Abbey, and I would not be needed. I think he knew I was a liberal and didn't want me under his supervision.

A few days later, he called me and said Father Omar could handle the ones who wet the bed, but they needed someone like me to work with the tough guys.

I talked it over with Father Tony, and he said go for it. I met the superintendent Ed Sidio, and he welcomed me aboard. I told him I would like to meet the whole population in an assembly, and he set it up. I stood in front of over a hundred young people from ages twelve to seventeen. I was only twenty-nine years old at that time and was in peak condition. Working on the farm and lifting weights in the seminary left me ready for anything. I announced my name as Father Tom, and I was there to learn from all of them and work with them to help them get back to making good choices, enjoying life, and helping others.

I then said, "Who is the toughest guy here?"

There was a stirring among the troops. Finally, someone said, "Chew-Chew." I told Chew-Chew to come up. Here came a big Native American young man, and I told him to relax, and I was not about to hurt him and whispered that I was going to pick him up and set him on the table that was near us. I told him quietly that I would hold him by his shirt and twist it gently and then take his pant leg and twist that too and then lift him over my head and do some body pumps. He smiled, and I did too. I said, "Ready," and he said, "Go for it, man."

I bent down and lifted him with my knees and my arms.

I did about six push-ups with him over my head and then set him gently on the table. I then turned to the open-mouthed group and said, "Now I am the toughest guy here." I said it was now time to use our minds and our skills and not to worry about who was the toughest and all that. I had a shirt with the clerical collar on, but I had no trouble working with the kids, and they all respected me, even the ones who were not Catholic. I worked with them all. One time, I had a conflict and had to change the time of our meeting. When I came next time, they were mad and said what was more important than our meeting. I said it was a funeral I could not change, so they then calmed down.

Father Tony was a very friendly person, and we were often invited to people's homes for dinner. When we were offered a drink, we never said no. Father Tony had a habit of shaking his glass with the ice cubes rattling when his drink was empty.

One time, I talked the Franciscan priest who said the Sunday10:30 a.m. High Mass into having him and me debate celibacy instead of a regular sermon. I used my work with ministers and rabbis who were married as my strongest argument. I think I won the debate because the young priest was not too sold on the idea of celibacy, even though he belonged to the Franciscan Order.

Having served as a priest for six years, I was beginning to look at celibacy in a new light. I was very active in the ecumenical movement. I had many interactions with Protestant ministers and Jewish rabbis. One time, the Baptist ministers refused to let the local rabbi say an opening prayer at the high school graduation because they felt that the Jewish faith did not accept Jesus Christ as the Son of God. At the meeting, I made a big deal out of that refusal. I said that one religion could not tell another what to believe. The rabbi was included in the graduation ceremony.

Most of the ministers and rabbis were married and had families. Again, most of them were working as hard or harder than many of the celibate priests I knew. A spouse and children did not prevent them in their work at all, and many helped keep them in touch with the problems that the average family was experiencing. I felt I should think the celibacy obligation through again.

Chapter 5

A Priest Resigns

My first move was to go back into history and study the reasons for celibacy in the Roman Catholic Church. While we were in the seminary, we did not study celibacy. It was a given if you wanted to be a Roman Catholic priest. We were told that being married would get in the way of serving people. You would not be able to be available 24-7. In a positive note, you were giving up a married relationship, so you could be totally dedicated to Christ and his church, God's people. It was a sacred sacrifice to show total dedication. No interference from a spouse and children. As I soon found out, it doesn't always work out that way, and it was a tough way to live it when you realized it was not necessary. It became unnecessary to lead a totally dedicated life. Other religions had people who married and still had total dedication to their vocation. In fact, all of us, married or single, can lead a life totally dedicated to helping others and still enjoy life itself. Priests seem to find other distractions to fill their day and nights (e.g., golf, tennis, cards, travel, alcohol, casinos, racetracks, season tickets for sports and theater, dine at four-star restaurants, drive nice cars, have hobbies, and other social activities to name a few).

One of our seminary professors of marriage, Monsignor John O, told the joke that two priests were talking when they overheard a woman arguing with her husband. One priest turned to the other and said, "Thank God for celibacy." At the time, we all laughed, but now it was no longer a laughing matter.

In one of our moral theology classes, our teacher Monsignor "Pinky" told us we should be wearing a cassock and surplice and light candles as we discussed sexuality. He went on to say that there are decent parts of the body (head, shoulders, hands, legs, and feet), less-decent parts (chest, hips, rear end), and indecent parts (genitals). I was ready to question the monsignor on the fact that God made all parts of the body, and they were all natural and good. To question the monsignor meant that you would probably be expelled. In my case, I could not afford the risk. One wonders why we did not go into celibacy in any depth after that introduction.

One of our jokes on celibacy was not to look down on the unemployed while we took our shower.

Celibacy initially stemmed from an ascetical impulse derived from early monasticism. The monks and nuns lived in monasteries and convents and were totally dedicated to prayer and God because many thought the world might be coming to an end soon, and they wanted to be ready for Jesus's second coming. It was a good bet that being a nun or a monk would assure you that you would go right to your reward in heaven, no purgatory, and be in your place with a high seat next to God for eternity. I know some in the religious life who still think that way. A nun once told us that when she gets to heaven, she is going to jump into Christ's lap and say, "Now, what do I get for all the sacrifices I have made?"

The monks also wrote by hand, making copies of all the scriptures and church documents. One of the jokes often told is the story of the monk who found out the word he was recording was *celebrate life*, not *celibate life*. They had been living the celibate life all this time because of a copying error.

In the Middle Ages, many bishops and priests were giving land to their families that had been donated to the church. It was a clear case of nepotism. Many people thought if they gave their property to the church when they died, they too would go straight to heaven. Local princes did not like it for the clergy to give donated property to their relatives. It was now a question of power.

In the eleventh century, many bishops, priests, and theologians engaged in wide spread debates for and against mandated celibacy. The First Lateran Council 1123, Canon 3, forbade priests to live with women (except relatives), and Canon 21 forbade the priest to contract marriage. The Second Lateran Council (1139) reaffirmed celibacy for the clergy. The history of abuse and property considerations won out, and the Roman Catholic Church made celibacy part of their human apparatus.

Note that the Maronite Catholic Eastern Rite, Greek and Russian Orthodox Churches have always had celibate and married clergy.

The New Testament tells us about the first apostles being married (First Corinthians 9:5): "Don't we have the right to take a believing wife along with us, as do the other apostles and the Lord's brothers and Cephas." We all know the story of Peter, the first pope, having his wife cured of a fever by Jesus (Matthew 8:4).

Late at night, after working a full schedule of Masses, funerals, preparing the Sunday and daily homilies, teaching in the grade school, meeting with the youth group, visiting the sick in the hospitals or in their homes, hearing confessions, preparing couples for marriage, witnessing weddings, visiting the local nursing homes and the Glen Lake TB Sanitarium, instructing new converts, counseling people with numerous problems, working with residents at the juvenile correctional facility and adult detention facility (jail), I would sit back with a can of beer and watch the end of the *Johnny Carson's Tonight Show*, knowing I would have to get ready for the 6:30 a.m. Mass the next morning and start all over.

Having seen and worked with my neighboring ministers and rabbis who were married, I said, "What am I doing?" Six years as a priest, I was happy, but not convinced I had to be not married and do some of the same type of work with people. Would the Roman Catholic Church change its position on celibacy in my lifetime? Looking at the history, I thought not. I was thirty-one years old, and the time to act was now. Thinking about celibacy in the seminary was one thing; living as a celibate alone for six years was another. Celibacy no longer felt like a necessary and reasonable sacrifice to me to be an effective priest.

I remembered again a friend of mine in the seminary, Hank Christenson, talking about never being a parent and having children or grandchildren and what a sacrifice that would be. I thought about that then but finally said it was one more gift we would be giving up as a celibate priest.

I finally decided to take my next step. It was to talk to two of my friends and tell them I was thinking of resigning the priesthood and going into corrections work full-time.

The first person I consulted was my classmate from St. John's University, Jack Quesnell. Jack had been in the seminary with me at St. John's and had left after one year. He was an excellent hockey player for the university and had gone into marriage counseling as a profession. I had sent many people to him over the years when they needed more technical counseling. Father Ray Monsour and I had worked for Jack years before at the Elks Youth Camp in Brainerd, Minnesota. Jack was a conservative Catholic, and he and his wife Alice worked together for years with Pre-Cana classes, preparing couples for marriage for the archdiocese. He would give me an honest, straightforward opinion. He did. He said he thought I was not making an emotional decision, but I had thought it out very well. He would like me to stay and continue my service as a priest, but he thought I was making a clear, thought-out decision.

My second stop was another friend of mine, Father Rufus "Ruf" North. He was the chaplain at St. Thomas University. He was a year behind me in the seminary, but he had a quick wit and keen mind and knew how to work with people. He too told me it was my decision, but I was doing it the right way. He wanted me to stay as a priest but respected my thinking. He too would leave the priesthood sometime later.

I then talked to my mother and told her my thinking. She had been a convert herself from the Lutheran Church when she got married and said the same thing about wanting me to continue my work as a priest, but first, she wanted me to be happy. She had been very active in our local parish and was a member of the Legion of Mary, which did a lot of charitable work in the community. I knew it would be harder for her. She remembered classmates of mine who left the seminary after years of preparation only to have their parents basically disown them. One of the assistants at our home parish, Father Paul, would later resign also.

My four brothers and their spouses were next.

My oldest brother, Ken, and his wife, Ellie, were not a problem. Ken knew the seminary from his days there, so he and Ellie were comfortable with my decision. He actually thought I would be wasted as a chaplain in a prison setting, a position I had considered asking for some time in the future. He was in law enforcement and thought I should work in the community. My feeling was that the people in prison were the people who needed my attention the most. But I did not want to start a position there and then leave them a short time later.

Next, my brother Ed was in the seminary for seven years, so he knew the ropes. His wife, Marilyn, was more traditional, but she did not protest.

Brother Dave and his wife, Irma, who was a convert, thought that priests should be allowed to get married anyway.

My youngest brother, Mike, and I went for a car ride as I told him about my thinking. Mike never did like the fact that I was in the seminary, much less ordained a priest. It put too much pressure on him and his lifestyle, so he was happy with my move.

I had to tell a few other close friends like Father Ray Monsour, Pat and LaVonne Mulvehill, Pete and Kathy Tobias, and a number of other friends I had gotten to know over the years. I didn't want them to hear it from someone else. I wanted them to know my thinking. I didn't want to sneak out in the middle of the night. I wanted to walk out with my head held high.

Our class was having a fifth-year class reunion, so at the end of dinner of the three-day celebration at a Minnesota resort, I made my announcement. The room was quiet for a long time. I heard that people were kicking one another under the table. Our classmate John was a bishop, and he asked me privately if I considered my friend Father Ray Monsour when I made my decision and that he might be left out in left field. I told him Ray was his own person, and he would still be my friend, and he could go on to continue his good work.

I asked my classmates to not publicize my resignation until after Labor Day because I would still be serving as a priest at the

Minnetonka/ Glen Lake Parish, and I had weddings that I had wanted to prepare and witness.

I then sat down with my pastor Father Tony Muscala and told him my plans. He was very supportive also.

People seemed to respect my request to not broadcast my decision.

All of a sudden, I was called into Archbishop Leo Byrne's office and told I was being recommended to be the new Catholic chaplain at the Minnesota Stillwater Adult Correctional Facility. He knew nothing of my plans to resign. Chaplain at the prison was a position I had always dreamed of, if asked. I could say Mass taped and have it played and replayed throughout the institution for inmates and corrections personnel. I could conduct adult classes and have them available in the local library and broadcast on the television sets if inmates and staff were interested. I could roam the population with a short-sleeve shirt and collar as a brother to all. I would even sleep in the cellblock on occasion. I could have general absolution daily and counsel any inmate who wanted to talk about their life. I could work with the inmate's family on the outside and hook them up with the community resources. I could help the reentry to the community for the inmate through jobs and other resources.

My uncle Chester and a first cousin had done time in Minnesota correctional facilities, so I could actually say my family was incarcerated just like they were. I could tell inmates and correctional staff that this was our community, our neighborhood, and we all had to work together to have decent living and working conditions so we could prepare for going back to our old communities. I would tell the mates who were "in" that what they did in prison would tell me what they would be doing when they were released. Live a better life now, and they would do the same when they were out.

As I sat before the archbishop, I told him about my grandfather, father, and brothers being in the law enforcement business and my other relatives who were on the other side. To my surprise, he told me that maybe I was not the right candidate for this job with my family history. I told him, on the contrary, I think I could do an excellent job. I had only one condition. He wanted to know what that condition was. I said I had studied celibacy and felt it did not have to be obligatory but optional. I felt I could be more effective as a married priest. I would be dating and eventually looking forward one day to the sacrament of matrimony and children and grandchildren.

To say he was speechless was an understatement. Obviously, he knew nothing of my plans. He finally said that condition would be impossible, and I should think this over very carefully. I said I had and talked it over with two counselors and had given it all the time it needed. I would be giving him now six months' notice in writing. I had prepared couples for marriage this summer and would like to witness their happy event. I told him I would resign the first Monday in September after Labor Day. I would not let my decision be known publicly until the Sunday before that date. He expressed he had no problem with that schedule. He asked me to go through a psychological test, which I did, and the psychologist passed me as being of sound mind. He said if my mind was made up, he would not stand in my way. Today a bishop would probably tell me to turn in my collar immediately. I told the archbishop I would apply to Rome to be released from any obligations to the priesthood. I often wondered if he was really glad to get rid of me, and the earlier offer to be the chaplain at the prison was a way to bury me in the belly of the beast. I must admit that he treated me well. I was one of the first to resign, and he would have many more to deal with in the future.

I could have kept my mouth shut and taken the job as chaplain, but I knew I was leaving, and I did not want to be working in the prison and all of a sudden leave the inmates and corrections staff hanging.

All went well, and the approaching day was drawing near.

Sunday, September 2, 1968, I had spoken to Father Tony Muscala and told him I wanted to speak at all the Masses and explain to the people my thinking and that I would resign the next day, Monday, September 3. He said he had no problem with me speaking. In fact, after I spoke at the early Mass, he followed me and said there would be a reception for Father Tom that afternoon from 2:00 to 4:00 p.m.

Father Tony did that after each of my sermons to his credit.

I began the first of my sermons by saying that I was called in by Archbishop Leo Byrnes and offered the position of chaplain at the Minnesota State Correctional Facility at Stillwater. There was an audible groan from the church pews. I went on to say that I would accept the position, although I loved the people of Immaculate Heart of Mary Parish, Father Tony, and the Glen Lake and Minnetonka community. Then I said I told the archbishop I had one condition and that I felt celibacy should be optional, and I felt I could do as well or better work if I could have a family and be married like my fellow ministers and rabbis.

There was another element of surprise from the congregation. People had said I was ahead of my time, which I took as a compliment. I knew that the Roman Catholic Church would not allow priests to marry in my lifetime, and so far, I am right.

That afternoon, hundreds of people came for my reception. Many said they were sorry to see me go, but they agreed that priests should have the option of celibacy or married life. They left envelopes with money, knowing that my transition from the priesthood to lay life would be difficult based on our low salary over the years. But I had saved since my teenage years and my mother's bookkeeping. I always wanted enough money to pay my bills and help out someone in need. When a parishioner could not pay for alcohol treatment, I could step up. I want to say that when I did that, they always paid me back. It may have been an incentive to make it through the program and stay sober.

Sunday afternoon, I packed up my meager belongings and headed for my mother's place. She had my grandmother Ernestine "Tina" Carney staying with her, so they both welcomed a man around the house.

I received many letters and notes wishing me the best. An example of one of the letters was from Ed Des Lauriers, a parishioner at Immaculate Heart of Mary Parish. It was sent to the archbishops Leo Binz and Leo Byrnes and auxiliary bishops Shannon and Cowley.

August 25, 1968
Archbishop Leo Binz
Archdiocese of St. Paul
And Minneapolis
226 Summit Avenue
St. Paul, Minnesota

Your Excellency:

It is a sad day for our family, and for most of the parishioners of Immaculate Heart of Mary Parish. Today we lost our assistant pastor, Father Tom Christian. You lost one of your best workers. And the troubled Catholic Church lost a fine Priest who applied his Christianity meaningfully and forcefully to the real problems of the modern world. We all lost him to a century-old celibacy canon that has little importance and even less purpose in today's times.

It's no personal tragedy to Father Christian, and certainly no moral disgrace to the Church. In his lay role, he won't lose his holiness, his Christian spirit, or his ability to inspire those who work with him. The real tragedy, of course, is that we have lost another dynamic priest to another antiquated and unimportant church law.

I pray that you will use your influence to bring about reforms in our Church's celibacy laws so you and I will not continue to lose good men and good priests we all need so badly.

Respectfully,

Ed Des Lauriers
Immaculate Heart of Mary Parish
Minnetonka, Minnesota

The only response he received was from Bishop James P. Shannon:

Aug.31, 1968

Dear Ed:

Thank you for your kind letter of August 25th. I
share your deep regret at the mutual loss in Father
Tom Christian's leaving the active ministry.
        I also share your view that the present legisla-
tion on clerical celibacy demands change. Let us pray.

Sincerely,

(Signed)
James P. Shannon

Sometime later, the St. Paul and Minneapolis Archdiocese chancellor was asked about the number of priests leaving the priesthood, and
his answer to the press was, "We have not lost any talent yet." A short
time later, Bishop James P. Shannon resigned. Bishop Shannon said the
reason he resigned was over the pope's encyclical stating that contraception be banned for all Catholics. He said he did not agree with it based
on his experience working with families in his parish. He did eventually
get married and did foundation work in Minnesota. I did receive a grant
from that foundation for one of my community corrections projects.
        I sent my request to Pope Paul VI to be released from any
obligations I had accepted when I was ordained a priest. I knew I
would need a positive response if I ever wanted to get married in
the Catholic Church. At that time, I had no animosity toward the
Catholic Church. I was not angry, but I knew they would not act
quickly on celibacy, and it might take a long time before they would
respond to my request. I was wrong, and I received the pope's reply
dated April 25, 1969. It would take about six months. Other priests
who wrote to Rome after me with similar requests had to wait for
long periods of time. Some would never receive an answer or were

told their papers were lost, or they were no longer giving any releases because they were trying to discourage priests from leaving. In one sense, I was lucky. I was early in my request, but then again, they were maybe saying, *Get this guy out of here as soon as possible*, not knowing there would be a lot more requests coming in over the years.

A translation of my rescript follows:

Most Holy Father

Thomas F. Christian, a priest of the Archdiocese of St. Paul and Minneapolis, humbly prostrate at the feet of Your Holiness, seeks a dispensation from all of the obligations flowing from Sacred Orders, not excepting the obligation of observing the law of holy celibacy.

The response from Rome:

Friday, April 25th, 1969:

His Holiness, Pope Paul VI, by Divine Providence Pope, after consideration of the recommendation of this plea presented by the Sacred Congregation for the Teaching of the Faith, has graciously decides that:

Thomas Christian is reduced to the lay state, with dispensation from all the obligations arising in Sacred Orders, not excepting the obligation of observing the obligations of observing holy celibacy, because of the lack of commitment, and without hope of readmission.

His Excellency the Most Reverent Ordinary of Saint Paul and Minneapolis will take care so far as he is able that the favors executed in such fashion as to avoid any scandal or wonderment on the part of the faithful. Therefore, before the favor has been utilized, he will make clear in appropriate fashion to the Petitioner that he must avoid completely those places where his previous status is known. The local Ordinary shall urge him to demonstrate his gratitude for the favor by leading an altogether exemplary life, by being an example to others, and by pursuing some work of piety and charity.

With reference to the canonical celebration of Matrimony, the Ordinary shall see to it that he refrain from any display and elaborate preparation, and that the marriage be performed in the presence of an approved priest bound by secrecy, and without witnesses—or if this be necessary, with two witnesses who are attached to the office of the Ordinary. Annotation of the ceremony shall be kept in the Secret Archives of the Diocese. In the baptismal registers of the parish of the Petitioner or of the spouse, annotation is to be made that the local Ordinary is to be consulted whenever some notice or document is required.

If some extensive concern on the part of the faithful should arise with regard to these matters, the Ordinary shall take care to offer an appropriate explanation of them.

This dispensation is granted without prejudice to it by reason of previous contrary actions, and is given at the offices of the Sacred Congregation for the Teaching of the Faith, on the 25th day of April, 1969.

The seal of the Tribunal of the Archdiocese of Sancti Paul is at the bottom of the Rescript.

Case: Christian, Thomas F.
Prot. Num.: S.C.D.F. 2495/68
S.P.A.M. 492/68

DOCUMENT OF ACCEPTANCE OF LAICIZATION

I, the undersigned THOMAS F. CHRISTIAN, now residing at 2201 West 69th Street, Richfield, Minnesota, 55423, hereby signify my free and willing acceptance of the dispensation from all of the obligations attached to Sacred Ordination and the religious life, graciously granted by His holiness, Pope Paul VI, on April 25th, 1969, and forwarded from the Special Commission of the Doctrinal Congregation on May 12th, 1969, under the Protocol Number 2495/68. I accept this dispensation recognizing that this acceptance is irrevocable, and I do so with the following understanding regarding 1) my future personal and spiritual life, 2) certain financial relational relationships, and 3) marriage.

With regard to my PERSONAL LIFE, I promise that I shall in every way strive, as the Rescript of the Holy See suggests, to be a SPECIAL EXAMPLE to all of piety and Christian charity. I furthermore agree that I shall so far as possible KEEP IN COMPLETE CONFIDENCE the fact of my having been ordained as a priest; in addition and to further this end, I agree to AVOID PLACES WHERE MY PRIESTHOOD IS KNOWN.

With regard to certain FINANCIAL ARRANGEMENTS, I hereby indicate that I understand that by acceptance of this dispensation I relinquish all claims, financial and otherwise, upon the Archdiocese or any of its components. I further agree that I shall discharge as soon as I conveniently can whatever outstanding indebtedness may remain toward the Archdiocese with reference to the costs of my seminary education.

With regard, in conclusion, to MARRIAGE, I hereby state my understanding and promise that out of regard for the current disquiet and understanding on the part of so many Christians in these matters, arrangements for a future marriage in the Catholic Church shall be made only through direct and personal application to the Ordinary of the place in which I may be staying or living, with the understanding that according to the conditions stated in the rescript of laicization, it be performed only in his presence or that of his delegate, with recording of the marriage to be made in accordance with the terms of the same rescript. A copy of the rescript is to be obtained on application to the Most Reverend Archbishop of Saint Paul and Minneapolis.

It is understood further that all publicity associated with such marriage will be regretfully declined, again against the possibility of misunderstanding and incomplete reporting.

I understand, lastly, that I relinquish completely all faculties and power of jurisdiction deriving from my Sacred Orders, and may under no circumstances simulate or attempt any use of them.

Executed at Saint Paul, Minnesota, on this 10th day of July, 1969.

_____

Thomas F. Christian

_____

Leo C. Byrne
Coadjutor Archbishop of Saint Paul and Minneapolis

_____

Terrance W. Berntson, Chancellor

When I met with Archbishop Byrne to sign the papers, I told him I did not lack a commitment to the priesthood, just a commitment to celibacy. I told him I had worked with ministers and rabbis who were married, and they did as good or better work than I was doing as a celibate. He said if I didn't sign the papers as written, I would not receive the dispensation. I told him I would sign the paper, but in my own mind, it was a protest against obligatory celibacy. He accepted my signature, and I was free at last.

Chapter 6

Beyond

I was no longer an active priest. In Latin, the term *Tu es sacredos in aeternum* means you are a priest forever according to the order of Melchizedek. They did not put that in the papers from Rome. I suppose in an emergency, I could still help people by absolving their sins with general absolution as the plane goes down. I hope that situation does not come up.

I felt good about everything, and I was ready to face the next challenges. I was not angry at the church or the hierarchy. I had many priest friends and lay friends. For the most part, they remained my friends. I was not alone against the world. I was ready to begin my new career.

Probation Officer

Months before, when I had decided to resign, I went to Ed Sideo, the superintendent at the Hennepin County Glen Lake Home School for delinquent juveniles where I volunteered as a Catholic priest counselor. I told him my decision. He and I had a good relationship, and I asked him if he had any openings for a full-time counselor. Unfortunately, he did not. His budget was limited, and if he could, he would hire me in a New York minute. However, he said they were accepting résumés for probation officers in down town Minneapolis. He said he would put in a good word for me, and I should take the test now.

Later, as I was writing the test, I looked up, and here comes a classmate of mine from Duluth, Minnesota, Pat McManus. He was a priest and principal at the local Catholic high school. He had also resigned and was taking the same test. We both passed with flying colors.

Pat was one of the smartest students in our seminary class and had also been trained in Rome. He was in line to become a bishop. Now the two of us were working with juvenile delinquents. Pat went on to become the assistant director of the Minnesota Department of Corrections and then the director of Corrections for the State of Kansas. He married and had a family but, unfortunately, died of Lyme's disease.

Our boss was Ken Young, assistant director of Hennepin County Court Services. He was a good Lutheran and would tell me later that if there were any other priests who wanted to resign, he would hire them, no questions asked. He said we were already well-educated, reliable, hardworking, and dedicated to serving people. I did recommend a number of priests who came our way, and true to his word, he hired them.

I was given six years' credit for my years as a priest, but the salary at that time was nine thousand dollars a year. It was the 1968 scale.

I was surprised after being on the job only a couple of weeks when my direct supervisor Jerry Benson asked me to give a community talk at a local school presentation on the role of a probation officer in the community. Here I was, brand-new and talking like a veteran. After preaching for six years, public speaking was actually fun.

They assigned me to South Minneapolis, including Central High School and Ramsey Junior High. It was one of the toughest areas of the city, and I loved it. I soon had a case load of 120 probationers. I hardly had time to learn their names. I started using volunteers to tutor kids and help them get summer jobs. I had one young probationer who quit school, never stayed home, and goofed off in his community doing minor crimes and giving everybody trouble. I talked to the school, and they said he was a bright kid but acted up and was kicked out a number of times and now was not going at all. I talked to his mother, and she said she could not handle him. I made the decision to bring him back to juvenile court and recommend he be sent to the Hennepin County Home School. I went out to visit him, and he told me that this was the best thing for him because he was on a crash course, and this saved him. It worked out for me too because the word went out to the rest of my caseload that if you don't shape up, Mr. Christian will ship you to a correctional facility.

Jerry Benson told me that he would continue to assign probationers to me until I howled, "Enough!" I worked with the hardcore kids and farmed the lightweight ones to volunteers after I gave them the word about making good choices and the consequences for goofing up. I kept in touch with all my probationers and tried to be as creative as possible with each one. I walked around the neighborhoods and informally talked to the kids I saw who were on probation. I also talked to teachers, neighbors, businesspeople in the area. Today they call it like community policing. It was done not only for surveillance purposes but to be known and an available resource.

One day, I was in Central High School checking on attendance and grades when two of the basketball players cornered me in the hallway. They had Afro haircuts and were called the "trees" because of their size. I was five feet nine and had to look up to them with a strained neck. They told me they didn't want me checking on their brothers, and I should get out of school and not come back. I told them no problem. I was making sure their brothers were doing the work in school and graduating, and I was working on getting them summer jobs so they had some money. But if they felt I should stand down and let them go to juvenile jail, I would let them know. They smiled and said, "Brother, you keep coming here, and we will back you."

Within a few months, I was promoted to senior probation officer.

Dating

Going out on dates was another matter. I was very shy and bashful as a grade school kid and grew up on a farm with four brothers. My experience with girls was rather limited. In high school and college and graduate school, I was in the seminary. I had gone out a few times with friends in the summer, and they would fix me up with a date. But I knew it was temporary, and not much was expected of me. My pastor had to report how I did all summer. I only went to church on Sundays because I worked every other day of the week. He always gave me a good report because he never heard anything to the contrary.

One time, I was in the back seat of the car, and my friends picked up two of their old girlfriends. One jumped in the back seat and started kissing me. For the ride to the party, she didn't stop. I went along with it, and on the way home, she started up again. I kept my hands around her and didn't try any other moves, and neither did she. I didn't know her and never saw her again.

Another time, one of the former seminarians fixed me up, and the girl sat tight next to me. But I was driving and enjoyed the ride and put my arm around her, but no other moves were made.

I was at group parties and dances, but they were tame compared to today's standards.

As a priest, I tried to be careful and be friendly, but not too friendly. One time, I was visiting a mother in the hospital, and her new baby was having medical problems. She was so happy to see a priest that she started to give me a hug. I stood still, and to this day, I wish I would have returned her hug. I didn't know her, but she needed a hug, and I was so careful I didn't respond.

There were times when women let me know they were interested in more than friendship or counseling. A number of women let me know in so many words that they were not happy in their marriage and may be open to a relationship if I was interested. I was very careful in those situations. I said to myself that as long as I was a priest, I was going to be on guard and play it safe. I overhead a couple of women talk about it being a challenge to snag me. It was not that I thought I was that attractive or handsome—although some women came right out and said I was. I was average height at five feet nine, and my hair was thinning. I made up for it with hairy arms and hair on my knuckles. I always said I was rotating the crop. I had long eyelashes that as a kid people would comment on, to my embarrassment. My personality was open and friendly. I had been educated to the nines, so I could carry on a conversation on most topics. I often saw women looking at me now, and I started to look longer at women. It was now fun.

As a priest, one of my best friends always wanted his wife to give me a hot kiss when we got together. I didn't resist that because he was right there and instigated it. I must say I enjoyed it, but it did not influence me to quit the priesthood.

A friend of mine once called me and told me that a friend of hers thought I was too friendly toward her, and I guess after thinking about it, I was. I called her as a priest and asked her to meet me. I told her that after two years as a priest, I could not develop more of a friendship; and until the Catholic Church changed its ruling on celibacy, our friendship had to be just that: a friendship. She said she understood. We did not meet again, and she married and went on with her life.

Another time, a married friend of mine asked if I loved her. She thought I was acting that way when we would be at a party. With her husband present, we talked about it, and he laughed. But I realized being friendly had to have more boundaries, and some people could misinterpret friendly behavior. Some women told me that it was a challenge to get the attention from a celibate priest. It was a safe relationship as long as it did not get out of hand. Most priests I knew were awkward with women, so I tried to be more human and friendly. I realized I had to back off that type of thinking.

Relatives and close friends were always greeting me with a hug or a kiss, so I was not starved for physical attention.

Now that I was available, things would be different.

Friends were coming forth with blind dates, as well as people I knew who were pointing out that I was now available as a thirty-one-year-old bachelor.

One young lady whose family I had known for six years and had a sister who taught at my first parish in Roseville was on my mind. I had been to their cabin in Northern Minnesota with the other assistant Father Hessian, and I was asked to witness her sister's wedding. I even had told some of my friends that if I was out there,

I would check her out. A couple of my friends did take her out. But they struck out. Now it was my turn. She was a nurse and worked at the Diabetes Center in Minneapolis, and I was in the hospital for the removal of a pianetal cyst. I told her I needed a nurse, and could she stop by and see me? I told her I was resigning as a priest and would like to take her out. She said yes.

The rest is history. She was the one back in the Bahamas in 1965 who saw me get into the fight over a chair. She was the one my friend almost gave a ring to. I saw her over the years at different events, so she got a more complete picture of who I was, not just another guy who thought he was tough.

Although we soon became a couple, she told me to continue dating to be sure that I was ready to begin an exclusive relationship. I did, but it only made me more certain that she was the one. I will not use her name in this book so we could keep our family relationship private.

My papers in Rome requesting I be relieved of any obligation to celibacy had come, so I was now able to be married in the Catholic Church. I went to my girlfriend's father with the papers in Latin and showed him the official document and translated the part that released me from any obligations. He and his wife were very good Catholics and went to Mass every day. I smiled when he said he always thought priests should be allowed to be married like other religious denominations. He gave me his blessing and approval to marry his daughter.

Marriage

We went to Dayton Hudson's department store to look for a ring. The person who waited on us was a former parishioner from Immaculate Heart of Mary in Glen Lake, Minnetonka. We knew the word would spread quickly. We designed the ring to have diamonds all around the circumference.

Wedding picture for Bernice and Tom Christian, who
were married on August 30, 1969 in James J. Hill chapel.
Only immediate family members could attend.

Bernice and Tom with Monsignor Ellsworth Kneal, a canon lawyer, who
was the official church and state witness for the private wedding ceremony.

We set the date for August 30th, 1969. My oldest brother Kenneth Christian would be the best man, and Bernice's sister Kathleen Ziegler would be the matron of honor. We were told by the chancery and Rome that we had to be married "quietly." No fanfare. We had to schedule the ceremony in the private chapel in the James J. Hill mansion next to the chancery in Saint Paul. No one could attend except immediate family. That meant even my long-time friend Father Ray Monsour could not be there as the papers from Rome stated they wanted to limit the scandal that a former priest was actually getting married in the Catholic Church. I think they also wanted to discourage other priests from thinking they could maybe make the same move. However, later history showed it did not work that way. Many priests started to leave.

The official minister for our wedding was the canon lawyer Monsignor Ellsworth Kneal. We met with him a week before the wedding, and we told him we wanted to write our own vows. He was very gracious and had no problem with our ideas. He actually asked us for a copy after the ceremony.

We had a gathering at Bernice's family home and then went to a private dinner at one of the St. Paul restaurants, Mr. Pedro's.

The honeymoon night was to be spent at a nice hotel called the Hopkins House in a suburb of Minneapolis. We had told them in advance we would be a late arrival, being married that day and with the dinner and all. We had reserved the honeymoon suite.

When we got there, we were told they had given our honeymoon suite away. I was dumbfounded. Welcome to the real world. They said they did have a studio couch available. It was a Labor Day weekend. I called downtown and got a nice room at one of the better hotels. When we got there, we found a Middle Eastern convention going on, so the noise was constant.

Before the honeymoon, I sat down with another former parishioner for whom I had gotten the job with the American Automobile Association, and we planned out the following two weeks. We started driving to Chicago, and once there, we went to a better planned hotel, one of the top plays and a great dinner. That was the city part of our adventure. Then we went to the Pioneer Inn in Oshkosh, Wisconsin, to enjoy the resort and relax.

Our final stay was at the Lutsen Resort in Northern Minnesota. I had set up horseback riding in a scenic area. Bernice said she had ridden before, so we went off. I was brought up on horses on the farm, so when we came to an open field I said, "Let's see how they run."

I looked back, and my new wife was hanging on to the saddle horn for dear life. She later then told me she had ridden once around a circle on a relatives ranch. We learned communication was an area we needed to work on.

After our honeymoon, my mother and family had a reception in her backyard, and Cyril Paul and his band, the Monarchs played. All our other family and friends were invited to this one.

One of our brothers-in-law went around saying the marriage would never last. If I quit the priesthood, I would soon get tired and quit the marriage too. We now have three grown children, five grandchildren, and we celebrate our fiftieth wedding anniversary in 2019.

Michigan State University

After a year as a probation officer, I knew I needed another degree if I wanted to move up the ladder in the corrections field. I sent applications to a number of schools to see if I could get in their graduate programs. It turned out that Michigan State University's School of Criminal Justice was one of the top schools in the nation. My brother Ken had gone there and encouraged me to apply. Ken was working on his master's degree too.

I was accepted and took an educational leave from Hennepin County Court Services. There were also law enforcement (LEAA) scholarships available. I was able to obtain funding, and my wife got a job in their School of Nursing on a multimedia project. We were in business.

We found a place to live above an older couple's home. It was so small that if we turned around in the kitchen, the gas stove went on. We burned out a teapot before we realized it.

One time, we came walking down the outside exit and saw a big possum in their garage. We thought it was a pet rat that had gotten away from one of the kids in the neighborhood. It was white with a long tail. After thinking about it, I determined it was a wild possum. It didn't take long to decide to move out of there.

It was time for my first test from my corrections class. *This should be a piece of cake*, I thought. There was only one question: Describe your thoughts on the continuum of the criminal justice system. I panicked. What did *continuum* mean? I sat for a few minutes and finally gave my ideas on the community, police, detention (jail), prosecution, courts, prison, and parole. I told my wife as she picked me up after the test that maybe I was too old to be starting school again. After all, I already had four years of high school, four years of college, and four years of theology. When I next went to that class, the professor said there was one A, and he handed me my test paper, and it was me. I told my wife, "I think I will stay in school after all."

My wife was now on the faculty for the School of Nursing, so we qualified for faculty housing. We had a faculty apartment for $120 per month, which included everything except our phone.

I attended a presentation by one of the PhD students on juvenile delinquency. It was one of my better moves. As the graduate student showed his statistics and talked about his findings, I asked a few questions based on my experience back in Minnesota. Afterward, one of the young professors came over and introduced himself. He was Dr. Robert Trojanowicz. He asked me about my work and said he was looking for a graduate assistant for his classes. I jumped at the chance and was soon teaching sections of his classes. I was thirty-one, and he was twenty-eight, so I had him by three years. He turned out to be a great friend, and he helped me for the next four years getting my master's and doctorate. We played softball and basketball in a Lansing City leagues. In softball, we played for Gino's Lounge and had pitchers of beer to celebrate our victories or drown our sorrows when we lost.

After I finished my master's degree, I applied for a Department of Justice fellowship and was awarded one to work on my doctorate.

The topic for my master's was "The Perception of Social Agency Personnel Toward the Police: A Study Conducted in Muskegon, Michigan" (1971). The results are even more interesting for today's criminal justice system with the police and the community. We found that the actual neighborhoods felt the police were not socially aware of the needs of their community. Bob Trojanowicz became a great advocate for community policing and published a book on the subject. Another result of the study found that social agencies and the police needed to work more closely to understand each other's function. There is a real need for interaction between all the resources in the community with law enforcement so the police don't see themselves as "us against them."

My doctorate was "The Organized Neighborhood, Crime Prevention, and the Criminal Justice System" (1973).

Once again, I tried to show that to depend only on the criminal justice system, crime will not be reduced unless communities get involved. This means neighborhood watches, neighborhood associations, school board involvement, volunteer police and probation officers, tutors, business associations promoting jobs and social agencies resources interacting with the communities. Low-income areas need community leaders to come forward and stand up for their communities.

One of the things we found was that black parents were not coming to parent-teacher meetings. The stereotype response was that the parents didn't care. We found the opposite was true. Many of the families came up during the great migration of blacks from the South and could not read or write. The answer was for the school social worker to visit the home and talk to the parents and start an adult education program to teach people how to read and write.

I do not want to go into too much detail on my studies, but my doctorate was 415 pages long.

When I was done with my study and had written the thesis, it was time to defend my work. The chairperson of my committee was none other than Dr. Robert Trojanowicz.

I had a person from sociology, one from psychology, and another person from the School of Criminal Justice. I was anticipating no problem. Right! The person in sociology, whose methodology I had used, decided I should set it all aside and look at it in the fall and, with a fresh look, make it even better. This was the middle of May 1973, and I was to report to Hennepin County Court Services for work in June 1973. Bob Trojanowicz to the rescue. He told me the same sociology professor had done that to him when he was defending his thesis.

He had told him to go fishing for the summer and then come back and take a fresh look at his thesis. He swallowed hard and told him he didn't fish. Bob told me to come with him and meet with the professor. We asked him what he thought should be improved. He made a few small suggestions, and I went home that night and made the changes. In a few days, we returned to the professor, and he approved my thesis.

Bob Trojanowicz promoted me a few years later to be on the Michigan State University School of Criminal Justice Alumni Board of Directors. I was able to then encourage the board to elect the first woman to serve on the board. Criminal Justice employees were traditionally mostly men. Now that is changing in the police and corrections fields.

A major event in our life while in graduate school was the birth of our first son on March 24, 1972. He grew up to be a mechanical engineer with a degree from Notre Dame. He had been a sprinter in high school and, for ten years, held the one-hundred-meter dash record at 10:8. He ran track for Notre Dame for four years and lettered. He ran with Raghib Ismaeil, "the Rocket," who went on to play ten seasons in the National Football League. I also like to say Craig is in the Notre Dame letterman's club just like Joe Montana.

He was in the Peace Corps for two years in Arsiniov, Russia. When he returned, he received a master's in environmental science from Washington State University and a law degree from the University of Seattle. He now lives in Seattle, Washington; and with all three of his degrees, he runs a beer pub called Rooftop Brewery. Stop by for a cold one. Tell him his dad sent you. He is married to Jessica Cohen, and they have a daughter, Abigail Rose, and a son, Elliott Frank.

Graduate school was a great experience for us, but it was now time to go back to work in Minnesota with our new son in arms.

Portland House

When I was getting ready to return to the Hennepin County Court Services, the now director Ken Young told me they had a special program that they wanted me to run. It was called Portland

House and was an alternative to incarceration for convicted felons between the ages of eighteen to thirty-five. These people had failed probation and were on their way to prison. The court would stay their sentencing, on condition they completed the Portland House program. If they failed here, they would be on their way to the big house (St. Cloud Reformatory or Stillwater Prison).

Ken Young said there was one condition I would have to agree to, and that was to become an employee of Lutheran Social Services. I said I would like to meet with the agency before I accepted the job. I told the director of Lutheran Social Services (LSS) that I had been a Catholic priest for six years in the St. Paul and Minneapolis Archdiocese, and I had my papers from Rome releasing me from any obligations, and would LSS have any problem hiring me? He said Martin Luther was a former Catholic priest, and they didn't have a problem with him and didn't see any problem with my background either. I took the job and was treated like one of the team immediately.

I ran the program for six years, and we were voted one of the outstanding programs in the entire country. After the first year, I hired a classmate of mine, another former priest, Norb Gernes. He and I worked together for six years when I took a job with the National Center for State Courts in Atlanta, Georgia. Norb continued to run the program. The program is running to this day.

There were four steps in the program. We first interview the candidates in the county jail. We then took them to the program and had the other residents interview them. If we all agreed they were ready to work on their problems, we recommended them to the judge who transferred them to us. Once in the program, I talked to them and told them it was up to them to get their act together and start contributing to our community. Were they tired of getting arrested and gathering dust in a jail cell? If they ran away from our open-door program, they were told they would be in prison, and they could blame no one but themselves. And five years could be added to their sentence. We then had them make their own bed and clean their room. We had them work in the kitchen and help the cook prepare the meals. They started on a healthy diet, so they felt better and soon would be ready to go to work in the community. Each evening, they attended group counseling. It was based on a peer-counseling model. A staff person facilitated the direction, but the peers helped each other, so there was no con trying to con a con. That was phase one. The next step was to prepare a résumé and practice interviewing for a job. An alarm clock was given to the candidate, and he had to wake up on time and get a good breakfast, learn the bus routes, and look for a job. We had employers who were ready to hire ex-offenders and give them a second chance.

The second step has the resident secure a job and stay with it. The tendency in the past was for the individual to quit his job if he didn't like the boss, or he had some money now and wanted to spend it as soon as he got it. In our program, the person had to talk out any problem at work with his group, and he was not allowed to quit unless the group approved. The person had to pay restitution to his victims according to a fair schedule. He had to pay taxes and family support. We worked with the family or significant other because they were often part of the problem as enablers or just dysfunctional. The resident had to meet with their group each weeknight and talk about their day and the reasons they were in trouble with the law.

The third step was to move out into an approved living situation and attend group meetings once a week.

The final step was to be on your own and report to your probation officer. If a person committed a new crime, they went to prison. If they quit or lost their job, they would have to come back to phase two.

We had a very good success rate. One-third worked the program as it was designed to work. One-third worked the program with their own style, but did not get into trouble again. One-third was not ready and went to prison. I would visit them there, and they would tell me that now they knew what they should have done. I told them they could begin again once they did their time and this time get it right.

1978: A Difficult Year

In 1978, our mother, Ruth, passed away on February 7. Our brother Dave suddenly died on May 1. My wife's father had heart failure in July, and our aunt Frances died in November.

Our mother had pseudobulbar palsy, sometimes called French polio, like Lou Gehrig's disease. For the last three years of her life, she was confined to a skilled nursing home. She could not swallow, talk, or move her arms or legs. Working at Portland House and being the boss, I could stop most nights on my way home for dinner and visit with her. We had a homemade card with the alphabet on it. We would point to a letter, and she would blink once for yes and twice for no. One time, she looked at the board, letting us know she wanted to say something. I picked up the cardboard and ran my finger down to *g*, and she blinked. Then came an *e* and a *t*. *Get*. We went on until she spelled out *that damn fly*. I looked up, and a fly was buzzing her face. I rolled up the newspaper I would read to her and swatted the fly. She smiled. I think she was suffering for all her five boys so God would be easier on us when it came time for each of us to go to the happy hunting grounds.

Our brother Dave had been in the military and, as I had reported back in Roseville and my first assignment, contracted spinal meningitis. He survived that, but he had an operation to clear his sinuses, and dormant pneumococcal caucus meningitis went from his chest up to his brain, and he lived for a couple of days and then died. The doctors failed to diagnose it. We later learned that penicillin would have knocked it out. He left his wife and three-year-old daughter.

My wife's father was eighty, and so was my aunt Frances. They had good long lives.

Two other years were also hard on all of us. On May 6, 2004, our brother Mike died of a heart attack. He had worked for Target and Gap stores. On June 16, 2009, our brother Ken passed away from Parkinson's and heart trouble. His wife, Ellen, had died from cancer five days earlier on June 11. Ken had been a police officer, state crime investigator, and finished his distinguished career as a professor in security issues for Michigan State University School of Criminal Justice.

The Minnesota Community Corrections Association

There were a number of programs to work with people in trouble with the law. There was federal, state, and local money available to address the needs of the criminal justice system. But the funding was beginning to run out. Programs were struggling to stay afloat. There were residential, day and evening programs, pretrial services, halfway houses, therapeutic communities, drug and alcohol centers, port projects like Portland House, special separate programs for Native American, blacks and women and mental-health-centered programs—all fighting for the same dollars.

We decided to form an association of all these programs to help one another survive. Gary Meitz, another resigned priest and classmate, ran a program for Hennepin County Court Services called the bakery for probationers. We went to each program and told them we either hang together or hang separately. Then we called a general meeting for all the programs, and we agreed to form the Minnesota Community Corrections Association. This would be a statewide organization and have dues and develop special training programs and standards.

We wrote a grant and received thirty thousand dollars from a local foundation, and I was elected president. Lutheran Social Services of Minnesota provided an office, and I continued to work at Portland House on a part-time basis. The idea worked, and we were able to have a united voice with federal, state, and local funding sources.

The year was 1979, and I was voted Minnesota Corrections Person of the Year. The association still works to this day.

The National Center for State Courts

There was an opportunity to spread our influence on alternatives to incarceration in twelve southern states, and I thought I would apply for the two-year grant from the National Center for State Courts southern office located in Atlanta, Georgia. The regional director was a man by the name of James R. James. I passed the interview and was hired. Portland House was now run by Norb Gernes, and we hired a top-notch person to run the Minnesota Community Corrections Association. I was technically on leave from Hennepin County Court Services again, so off we went to "Hotlanta."

On October 4, 1974, our second son was born in Minneapolis. He too was a track star in high school and qualified in the two hundred meters for the New York State meet and then went on to run and letter at Lafayette College in Eastern, Pennsylvania. As a junior in high school, he won the two-hundred-meter regional race; and that evening, he went to the junior prom and was elected King of the Prom. I told him this may be one of the best days of his life.

Andy now teaches math in Tucson, Arizona, and was the track coach. To spend more time with his sons, now he only coaches the cross-country team. He is married to Paula Vargas, and they have two sons, Anderson Thomas and Beckett Jon.

August 5, 1977, our daughter Jen was born, and she too ran track, played soccer in high school, and went to Georgetown University majoring in foreign service. She has a master's degree in

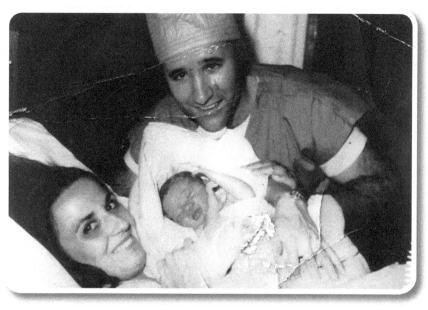

Bernice and Tom at the birth of their daughter,
Jennifer. Tom was able to be in the delivery room
when all three of their children were born.

international public health from Tulane University and has worked in China for six years and now has a position in her field in South Africa. She is married to Brandon Gassner, an architect, and they have a young daughter, Audrey Amelia, named after two strong women, Audrey Hepburn and Amelia Earhart.

So it was with three children, my wife and I moved to Atlanta, and I began working in the twelve southern states promoting alternatives to incarceration. We worked with judges and local criminal justice personnel, especially on restitution centers and neighborhood justice centers, along with all our ideas from our Minnesota experience.

We ended our two-year grant with a conference, inviting people from all twelve southern states.

One of the members of the board of directors for the National Center for Courts southern office was the chief judge from the New York State Unified Court System, Lawrence J. Cooke. When I

Tom with son Andy, daughter Jen, and son Craig. Tom played softball into his sixties. He was an all-state centerfielder for the Knights of Columbus league.

gave my final presentation to the board, he approached me and asked what was my next project. I told him I was going back to Minnesota to work for the courts there. He said he wanted me to come to New York and start a community dispute resolution centers program for him. They had sixty-two counties in New York, including the five boroughs in New York City, and he wanted a state-wide program using conciliation, mediation, and arbitration to relieve the overburdened courts across the state.

Tom with son Craig who, as a joke, is buried in sand up
to his neck on the beach at St. Simon's Island.

I contacted Ken Young back in Minnesota and asked him what was available as I was completing my project in Atlanta. It was 1981, and he said the economy was hurting, but he would find me "something." That didn't sound too promising. The chief administrator for the New York Unified Court System said I would have to live in New York City if I took their job. My wife said she would not want to raise three kids in the Big Apple, so I told them I would not be available. But the chief judge Lawrence J. Cooke said he wanted me to start the project, and I could live in the New York Albany area. That was 150 miles from New York City. It meant I would be centrally located, but I would have to travel to New York City often. There were Amtrak trains running all the time, so it looked good. My wife said she was on board, and we were off and running.

The New York State Unified Court System

We moved into a new home in Glenmont, New York, a suburb of Albany. I was ten minutes from work, had a state car, a parking spot underground, and didn't drive into the sun to or from work. I had a good salary, hired three great workers; and each summer, I was able to take three weeks off and go to Minnesota to our lake cabin in Avon ninety miles from the Minneapolis, the "mini-apple."

I worked in a great atmosphere for fifteen years. We developed community dispute resolution centers in all sixty-two counties including the five boroughs in New York City and handled twenty-five thousand criminal, civil, and family cases a year. We trained volunteer citizens to serve as mediators in their communities and even had a victim-and-offender mediation program.

I was able to mediate myself a case of a person seriously shot in a robbery, and it was filmed in prison with their permission on HBO television. We also had a case on *48 Hours* television program between a drunk driver and the mother of a young daughter who had been killed by him in a car crash. We also had a mediation aired by National Public Radio of a robbery involving a shooting. All these mediations were filmed or taped with all the party's permission, and we used them for training purposes and public-speaking presentations.

In the HBO film, the victim forgave his shooter; and after serving his minimum sentence of twelve and one-half years, the victim asked that the person be released on parole. We then had the three of us go around to high schools to talk about making the right choices in life. We even spoke at the Albany Law School. My part was to talk about restorative justice and how the victim gains information, healing, and closure; and the offender takes responsibility for his or her behavior and is able to express remorse to the victim for the crime. The young people were all eyes and ears, and more than once, a high school student would tell us that he was going to quit school early but decided that, based on our presentation, he was making the smart decision to stay in school and graduate.

When New York State offered an early retirement, I was ready. As you remember, our father had died at age sixty-one, two months before his retirement. I had always said I would retire at fifty-nine and one-half if I could. I was at fifty-nine, looking to retire in March 1967. They gave me fifteen months' extra credit with my fifteen years of service. And fortunately, I had never been sick, so I had sick leave that could go toward my health insurance for the rest of me and my wife's life. I retired November 1, 1996.

The Tres Amigos, brothers Ken, Ed, and Tom, in Mexico.

Bernice and Tom hiking in Arizona.

Bernice and Tom hiking in the beautiful, wind-shaped
Coyote Buttes on the Utah/Arizona border.

Bernice and Tom participating in the local community variety show. Bernice sang and Tom was Master of Ceremonies as W.C. Fields.

Bernice and Tom will celebrate their 50th anniversary in 2019.

The Bernice and Tom Christian Annual Family Reunion.

They had a nice retirement for me. Our dispute resolution centers program directors came from all sixty-two counties. Some people, especially judges, were surprised that I went out that early. I had just completed developing a court dispute referral system for the New York City courts and chief city court judge Robert Keating, so I had done what I had come to do. Mark Collins, my assistant, had been with me for fifteen years, so he was willing and ready to take over the reins.

My wife was working as the nurse educator for Wildwood's homes for adults with disabilities, and she decided to work one more year. That gave me time to write a book for the American Correctional Association on conflict management and conflict resolution in corrections. I had made the mistake of asking their publication department if they had anything on conflict management, and when they said no, they said, "Why don't you write something on that?" So I did, and it was published in 1999 and became a bestseller. Years later, they asked me to revise it, and they published the new edition in 2014.

I now had some time to do some training in victim-and-offender mediation. I used the films from HBO and *48 Hours* in the training. I was asked to write up the mediation from HBO by a number of our trainees. With the help of the victim and the shooter, I wrote up the story. It was published by Ink Water Press and is used by a number of university criminal justice classes as a case study. It was used by the victim as he continues to give a number of presentations on his own to schools and other interested groups.

The victim-and-offender dialogue is still being utilized by the community dispute resolution program and the New York Department of Corrections.

After a year of doing training and writing, my wife decided to retire also. We looked at retirement areas in Florida, North and South Carolina, and Arizona. We liked Tucson, Arizona, the best and moved there in 1998. We return to live five summer months on a lake in Minnesota. We have the best of both worlds. Tucson has mountains and 89 percent sunshine; Minnesota has ten thousand lakes. We have family and friends in both places.

In retirement, I am able to look back and comment on the present situation in the Catholic Church. My first thought was to write a letter to Pope Francis.

Chapter 7

A Letter to Pope Francis

Having been a Catholic all my life and a priest for six years, I was very happy to see Pope Francis come into the picture.

As I said, I was not angry at the Catholic Church as some priests, nuns, and brothers who resigned were. I was disappointed in positions the Church had taken in a number of areas. I was very disturbed by the number of religious who were involved in pedophilia and other sexual behavior that was a crime, and the hierarchy who tried to cover it up. I was also concerned about the conservative direction the Catholic Church was going and the number of far-right priests and bishops who were perpetuating a very narrow approach to living a good Christian life. Many of the new priests being ordained are actually being called "John Pauls" after the very conservative pope from Poland.

I served as a lector at our local church, but I did not tell them my background. They used me about twice in seven months, so I finally did not sign up anymore.

Rather than just complaining about the Catholic Church, I sat down and decided to write to Pope Francis the following letter:

Pope Francis
Vatican City, Italy
February 14, 2014

Dear Pope Francis,

Many of us are delighted that you are breathing
fresh air into the Roman Catholic Church and
redirecting the emphasis to serving the poor and
needy. The Church has been said to be regressing
back into a far-right, conservative, exclusive institution; and to some others, it is ready to go into
hospice. Here are a few suggestions that you may
want to consider to continue to bring the Church
back to life and into the twenty-first century.

The Role of Women

You talked about the role of women being
increased. The first thing you may want to consider is having women ordained as deaconesses,
so that should not be a problem justifying. We
realize that some people fear that if you ordain
women as deaconesses, the next step is to ordain
them as priests. But go one step at a time.
Jesus had twelve apostles, all men, but today, if
Jesus were picking his apostles, would he be an
equal-opportunity employer? We think so.

Divorced Catholics

Statistics show that a large number of marriages
end in divorce. A Catholic who is married in the
Church and later goes through a divorce cannot get married in the Church unless he or she
receives an annulment. That means they are told

if they marry again, they must go outside their church to declare their love to each other and be married, and they should not go to communion to receive the bread of life and remain together. The fact is, they should be allowed to marry in the Church. Would this cause more Catholics to seek divorce if their married love no longer exists? Should they stay in a relationship that is broken?

Christian marriage is a sacrament that should be allowed to all who believe in it. It appears that the Church is trying to stop people from getting divorced too easily, but it is causing more pain and suffering instead of keeping families together.

The Sacrament of Penance

The sacrament of penance or reconciliation should be available as a community absolution at the beginning of each Mass, as well as a separate ceremony. If people want to confess their sins individually and receive advice, that should be their choice. Is that making it too easy for sinners? Does the fact that you committed a mortal sin keep one from committing the sin because they have to now go to confession? It may, but is that good reasoning for intelligent people today? When people down through the centuries could not read or write or think for themselves, did the Church keep them afraid and in line?

Each person has to make that behavior choice for their own peace of mind. A person should be able to be renewed often in her or his efforts to live a better life.

Celibacy

As pointed out, the preparation for the priest-hood should be monitored so, in your own words, "monsters" are not ordained. Today too many candidates are attracted to the priesthood because it is a safe haven for people who have problems with their sexuality. Being not allowed to marry fits their problems to a tee. Therefore, celibacy should not be mandatory but optional for parish priests and nuns who will be working with children, women, and men of all ages. As the Protestant ministers, Eastern-rite churches, and rabbis have proven, it is more natural for people to be married and, if they wish, to be parents.

Celibacy goes back to the eleventh century and was started by monks in the monasteries. Bishops who were married were getting too pow-erful and giving land to their children and rela-tives. The powerful princes wanted to stop this nepotism and keep the clergy in line. For monks and nuns in the monasteries, it made sense to dedicate yourself totally to God, particularly when you thought the world was soon coming to an end. It has always been a struggle down through the ages for priests, brothers, and nuns to truly live the life of a celibate.

Sermons

In the training of priests, more emphasis should be on preparing and delivering meaningful ser-mons. Today, too often, holy words are strung together and have no application to the needs of the person in the pew. Focus is often only on the liturgy itself doing all that is needed.

Contraception

Being responsible parents, most Catholics plan
their families and practice birth control. If contraception is approved in a positive way, will
this cause people to be promiscuous? That again
should be their decision.

Abortion

The emphasis by the Church should be on education and responsible sexuality. To be against
contraception and abortion takes away from people having an alternative. If some people believe
that a fetus is not a human being until the fetus is
viable, that should be their choice. A miscarriage
is not considered a viable fetus by nature. God,
ultimately, will take care of all his children.

Thank you for your time and consideration of
these ideas. People who have left the Church,
both young and old, may be willing to come
back if some of these suggestions are introduced.

Sincerely,
Thomas Christian, PhD
Social scientist, retired

(As of yet, I have not received a reply. Word is that Pope Francis
is looking into bishops in South America who are running into the
problem of a shortage of priests and is ready to tell them to ordain
married men, and he will be willing to approve their decisions.)

Chapter 8

Thomas, the Doubter—I Think, Therefore, I Doubt!

This final chapter is composed of a number of questions. Some of them I have touched on in the other chapters. They are matters I have thought about over the years, and many are not answered and may never be. I hope I do not upset traditional Catholics too much, but you have been warned: this is a book by Thomas the doubter. No, I have not lost my faith. Thomas Aquinas states, "To one who has faith, no explanation is necessary. To one without faith, no explanation is possible." I prefer to say I have more hope than faith in some of the things we have been taught over our lifetimes. I also hope I practice more charity to make up for my doubts about some of the items under the category listed as faith.

Doubt is part of faith. Indifference is the opposite of faith.

I am anything but indifferent. I question a number of things, and I doubt some of them are true as we were taught over the years. I do not have "blind faith," as you can see. Some people accept items of faith and say it is a gift from God. Those are the areas I still have questions on.

The Spirit of the Law Over the Letter of the Law

I agree with Pope Francis that we should be looking at life with the spirit of the law and not the letter of the law. I write the following comments with this philosophy. An example of the letter of the law is the Church's stand on Catholic marriage. It states that marriage is a sacrament, and marriage is forever. "Till death do us part." However, many Catholics get divorced and want to marry someone else. The letter of the law says they cannot get married in the Catholic Church. They cannot go to communion if they do get married again. They can go to church and just attend. The spirit of the law says that because between 45 to 50 percent of people who marry get divorced (National Survey of Family Growth), therefore, the Church should lighten up and recognize that the old marriage is over, and a new love relationship should be seen as a sacramental marriage. The reason the Church does not want to change this area may be that they want the family to stay together, and divorce and remarriage made too easy will increase the number of divorces. But do we really want people to stay in an unhappy marriage and suffer? They often do not, and the Catholic Church is not doing them any favors by putting them on the fringe of the Church. If marriage is a sacrament and helps make people grow in their relationship, shouldn't the Church give people who are divorced this opportunity too?

The First Question: Is There a God?

A basic question that has to be answered as we start this section on doubt is, is there really a God? My first reaction is, can there be a God who allows children, young people, and adults of all ages to be killed in war, acts of terror, disease, and other tragedies down through the ages? Many have never had a chance at life. What about people with severe disabilities? Their lives are often shortened and limited. Therefore, there is doubt that there is a God.

But on the other hand, I can't believe that the world just happened. There is too much beauty and diversity for just a blind evolution. Aristotle says, "In all things of nature, there is something of the marvelous." The human mind is something that had to have a creator. Therefore, I think there must be a "Mind", or better yet, a "Being" behind all this. Is there a profound truth that lies outside of science? Is this Being, God? Yes. God is not a "divine being." That would limit God. God is "Being" itself. God gives us life and lets us make our way the best we can. We can thank God for all we experience in life. We can thank God each day for all the beauty of creation. We can thank God for the gift of love. In experiencing love in its many forms, we are closest to God.

I don't think God is going to intervene in our every move or keep a book on our behavior, and on judgement day, we will find out if we will make it to heaven or spend the rest of eternity in hell. How about if we just miss making it to heaven? Think about it.

God does not find us a parking spot because we pray to God. We are on our own to live our life as we work and live our lives. We can thank God each day for all we experience in life. It may be in a life as a nun or a monk or a single person or married. How we live our lives and love is thanking God. We can appreciate this "Being" and acknowledge this "Being" each in our own way. Some will go to organized worship, others will be on their own, and some will not believe in this "Being "at all. We are *human beings*. We are made "in the image and likeness of God," who is Being itself (Genesis 1:34). When we die, we will join God in the eternal "Being." We will be on the level according to how we lived our lives. *Mirabile dictu* (marvelous to relate)!

Is Jesus the Son of God?

Our family name is *Christian*. I always saw myself as a follower of the teachings of Jesus Christ. We are all sons and daughters of God. Jesus is our brother.

There are some other points in the New Testament that are attributed to Jesus that I have problems taking as good advice. Read Luke 14:26, Luke 18:29–30, Luke 9:59–62, Luke 12:51–53, Matthew 19:29, Matthew 8:19–22, Matthew 10:34–37, Matthew10:21, and Mark 10:29.

In those passages, Jesus tells us to hate our family members; let the dead bury the dead; he did not come to bring peace but rather division; and brother will betray brother, and a father his child; and children will rise up against parents and cause them to be put to death.

I prefer the Jesus who says to love one another in John 13:34. We were taught that because Adam and Eve sinned in the Garden of Eden by eating the forbidden fruit, God had to send his only Son to come to earth to save us. If the story of Adam and Eve is just a story to help explain the beginning of humanity, then did God have to send Jesus to die on the cross to save us? I mention this not to question whether Jesus is the Son of God but to have people think and come up with their own answer. Followers of Christ is just one of the many Christian religions, but the belief in a God in some form is in many other religions. I am a Christian and follow many of the teachings of Christ. I do question that he has to be the Son of God. I believe he was a very holy person and taught us how to be better people. Was he raised from the dead? I don't think he had to be raised from the dead. I still do not think I have lost my faith in God or in humanity. I do not doubt, but like St. Thomas has questions on some issues, so do I.

Is the Roman Catholic Church the One True Church?

There are many religions in our world. According to the *World Christian Encyclopedia: A Comparative Survey of Churches and Religions from 30 AD to 2000*, there are 19 major world religions, which are divided into a total of 270 large religious groups and many smaller ones. Some estimate there are 4,200 religions in the world. (World Religious Statistics, March 5, 2015.) Even Pope Francis said there are many ways to go to heaven. Just think of the many Christian churches, the Jewish religion, Buddhism, Hinduism, Islam, Native American beliefs, to name a few. Yes, the Roman Catholic Church can trace its origin to Peter, the first pope, and all the popes up to Pope Francis. Some of those popes were nothing to brag about. For example, Pope Alexander VI (1431–1503) had seven illegitimate children with his many mistresses. Pope John XII (937–964) was killed by a jealous husband, and Benedict IX (1012–1065) sold the papacy for a large sum of money so he could marry and then tried to get it back. Then there were the crusades (1096–1487), fighting the Muslims to recover the Holy Land and the twelfth-century Inquisition to punish and often kill those who did not follow the Catholic Church (heretics). The Catholic Church has done some terrible things in the name of religion. The hierarchy in our own time does not come off too well either. For example, the movie *Spotlight* won the Academy Award as Best Picture in 2015, showing the role of the Catholic Church in hiding clerical abuse of children.

What Is God Going to Do with All These People at the End of Time?

This is one of the theological questions I have as I read history down through the ages. Billions of people so far! As I watch people in Walmart and other places, I wonder, will all these different people fit in heaven? I have traveled all of the fifty US states and thirty-four countries and marvel at the numbers. For example, India has a present population of 1.2 billion, and China has 1.3 billion, and that is only counting today's population. I know that heaven must be infinite. Maybe people will be on different levels of "Being" with their involvement dependent on their faith and good works. Will the people we know be on our same level? And what are we going to do after we see our family and friends? Stand there and make small talk, and what happened to Uncle Charlie the pedophile? I don't think we have to worry about what God is going to do with all of us.

Is There Really a Heaven and a Hell?

We certainly hope there is a heaven, but is there a hell where people will suffer forever? The Church has scared us for sure, but heaven, I can hope for, but I can't see a hell. Maybe people who don't make it to heaven will go into a type of zone or "being" where they can't experience anything except a long sleep forever. That would be a hell in itself. They never loved enough in life, so their spirit will be unconscious in the great beyond. People like Hitler or Stalin are history and will never surface again.

What about the babies who didn't make it to childhood? What about the teenagers who died before they had a chance to reach adulthood? What about the billions of people again who died in wars, terrorism, weather extremes, or from diseases? What about the person who was born with a severe handicap? They will be in heaven, no doubt, without any disability.

My hope is greater than my faith in there being a heaven.

I doubt there will be a hell with fire and brimstone. What prevents us from doing anything we want to do if there is no hell? To enjoy life is not a problem. To hurt others is a problem. We should strive to enjoy life and help others to join us in making a better place for all of us. Will God reward us? We will reward one another, and that is what God wants us to do.

What About the Bible?

Many parts of the Bible have some great advice. Other parts don't sound like the inspired Word of God. They sound like the ideas of old men. Should the slave be obedient to the master? (Psalm 123:2, Malachi 1:6, Colossians 3:22). Should the wife be obedient to her husband? (St. Paul to the Ephesians, chapter 5). Should parents take their disobedient children to the outskirts of town and stone them? (Deuteronomy 21:18–21, Leviticus 20:9). Most of the stories in the Bible are made up to answer basic concepts for people. I don't think God whispered all these ideas into the ear of the writer. Therefore, I doubt the Bible is inspired by God. It is the writings of people who thought they were inspired by God. Does this make the Bible less worthy of our inspiration? No. We should see the Bible as one of the great books down through the ages, and if it helps people to live better lives, more power to it. But I don't think we should take it literally.

For example, the story of Adam and Eve is an attempt by early writers to explain the beginning of human beings. Was there really a Garden of Eden where the first couple ate the forbidden fruit? How did they multiply as a race if Abel was killed by Cain? I visited the Maropeng Museum in South Africa, the cradle of humankind. There, it is demonstrated that humans are over a million years old. I believe in evolution. God was our Creator who gave us being, and we have existed as a race for centuries.

What About the Idea of the Trinity?

The word *trinity* is not in scripture, nor is there an expressly formulated doctrine of the Trinity. In AD 325, the Council of Nicaean adopted the term in the Nicene Creed. I always have had my doubts about the concept of the Trinity. God is God. A learned priest who taught in the seminary once said, "Don't try to figure out the Trinity—the Father, Son, and Holy Spirit. Just accept it as faith."

What About Original Sin?

We were taught way back in grade school that because Adam and Eve ate the forbidden apple in the Garden of Eden, we all had to be baptized to have the original sin washed off our soul. We inherited it from our first parents, an ancestral sin. It was first alluded to in the second century by Irenaeus, bishop of Lyon. This was the story that was developed by people like St. Augustine (354–430), St. Anselm (1033–1109), and St. Thomas (1225–1274) and handed down through time. The question I always asked myself was, it did not seem fair to all of us if the story of Adam and Eve was really just a story, or did it really happen? I doubt we were handed down original sin. And after Cain and Abel, where did all the rest of the people come from? It even questions whether Jesus had to sacrifice his life to save us. He may have been a man of God who showed us how to live our life. Many non-Christian religions hold that Jesus was one of the great prophets but not the Son of God.

Why Are There So Many Priest Pedophiles and Sexual Abusers?

Yes, there are ministers who are sexual abusers, and on occasion, a rabbi may be exposed, but it is nothing compared to the number of priests who have been identified around the world as molesters. It is an international problem for the Catholic Church. Just in the State of Minnesota, there have been sixty-six priests in the Archdiocese of St. Paul and Minneapolis who have been named as abusers. At St. John's Benedictine Abbey in Collegeville, Minnesota, there have been twenty monks on the list. These are only two areas in Minnesota, and this does not include all the dioceses.

The magazine *The Economist* (August 18, 2012) says there has been 3.3 billion dollars in settlements over the past fifteen years by the Catholic Church. That number is rising annually with bankrupt-cies and lawsuits pending.

The New York Archdiocese has released a report, December 7, 2017, paying $40 million to 189 identified people who are victims of clergy sex abuse. The payouts averaged $211,600.

Is obligatory celibacy one of the reasons for the high numbers of priest abusers? Yes, according to a study in Australia by the Truth, Justice and Healing Council on December 12, 2014, and reported by the *National Catholic Reporter* (NCR), January 2, 2015. Celibacy itself is not the problem. A person can be celibate and live a very ded-icated life. Obligatory celibacy can be a problem. Celibacy is taken by a seminarian when he becomes a subdeacon. Should he know what he is doing? At that time, he maybe does; but later, as a priest, he finds it very lonely and takes to other distractions like travel, costly restaurants and entertainment, drinking to excess, or he can begin to act out sexually often when he has been drinking.

Celibacy also causes many very good candidates to not choose to be priests because they want to be married and father children and live a normal, natural life.

As a social scientist by education (PhD, Michigan State University, 1973) and also as a priest for six years and having talked to and observed some of the priests who have been accused, I believe there appears to be three types of priest abusers who have been reported on in the press. First is the pedophile. This is a person who abuses children. He can control and frighten them. He is addicted to this behavior. He rationalizes that he is expressing his love in a twisted way and is not doing any long-lasting harm to the young child. He is physically, mentally, and emotionally satisfying his addiction.

Little was known about this behavior even by the so-called experts. It was kept quiet except for notorious cases, and then the person was sent to prison, where he was at the bottom of the totem pole and at risk from other offenders.

For example, the case of John Geoghan was notorious. He abused children right after he was ordained and was moved often for years. He was finally convicted to serve eight years in Souza-Baranorsi Correctional Center forty miles northeast of Boston. Shortly after his confinement in 2004, he was strangled by thirty-seven-year-old inmate Joseph L. Druce, who belonged to a white-supremacy group.

But this was not the case for most priests. Priests were sent to professional counseling programs, many times for months. Often, they were returned so-called cured and put back into ministry, only to offend again. Many were called in to the chancery and questioned. Then they were just sent to another assignment with no treatment to act out again. Authorities thought the person had learned his lesson and hopefully would not offend again. The archbishops, bishops, and other religious superiors wanted to protect Mother Church from scandal and being sued. They and the professionals did not understand the addiction that causes pedophile behavior. This is not an excuse because this type of behavior is a crime, not just a weakness, a sin, or a sickness. It should be reported to the police for possible arrest and to the district attorney for prosecution.

The victim was given limited consideration and often not believed. It should be noted that, on occasion, it was discovered by the police, and they too did nothing or just told the local pastor or religious authority. It was considered a local church problem and should be dealt with on that level. They did not want to deal with it in the normal criminal way and make an arrest.

Pope Francis has decided that any appeal after treatment to a proven abuse case, the person will not be allowed back into ministry. The pope did allow a case back into active ministry, and the person offended again. Even the pope now realizes that the abuse is an addiction.

Secondly, there is the person who is homosexual and is attracted to young boys, usually in their teenage years. The homosexual priest or brother—just as the bisexual, heterosexual priest or brother—has to control his feelings toward the same or opposite sex; and if he is to be a true celibate, he cannot act on those feelings. Temptation, we were told, is not a sin. By the way, nuns, both lesbian and heterosexual, have also been recorded in this category, but not to the extent that priests were involved.

Thirdly, there is the priest who does not keep within the required boundaries with women, young and old. First, there is flirting, and then a friendly hug that leads to a kiss, and finally, actually sleeping with them. This too is a crime if they are supposedly giving them spiritual counseling or the girl is still underage. The reporters who did the investigation for the movie *Spotlight*, exposing the cover-up in the Boston Archdiocese, are now looking into the children of priests and the problems surrounding this area.

Many people who have sexual problems are attracted to the religious life. It is a safe haven with instant status. No one would question a priest who was supposed to be celibate until he was reported to the bishop. This often was kept secret and not even written up in a file but kept on the verbal level or limited notation. Information was never passed on to the next assignment. No one wanted to sabotage a person's future or career opportunities. They were told not to do that kind of behavior again.

Then there were the cases of the gay priest. As long as he was discreet and had a cooperative partner, there was no action. The gay priest figured the Church was behind the times and again rationalized that his relationship was fine. Many priests have a particular female friend and, for the same reason, rationalize that even sexual relations can be okay. After all, what is the problem with having friendships? If they end up in a sexual relationship, particularly with a married woman, they are now in the adultery category.

Optional celibacy is needed just for natural feelings to be shared in a marriage where two people can have a healthy relationship.

There were often two types of candidates for the priesthood: one was the all-American young man who was out to save the world, and the other one was in love with the ceremony, the incense, and status surrounding the role of a priest.

The religious life is often seen by ministers, rabbis, and priests as restrictive and limiting. A person finally can go off the deep end. That may be why a minister falls off the wagon, so to speak, and has a sexual encounter with someone who is not his wife, or the person is underage. He is then repentant and even cries out that he is a sinner, as we have actually seen on television.

To conclude, there are many reasons why a priest is accused of sexual abuse: obligatory celibacy, personal sexual problems coming into the priesthood, restrictive lifestyle, loneliness, depression, lack of proper boundaries, uncontrolled homosexual or heterosexual tendencies, and limited consequences for their behavior. They used to be able to get away with it for years, and therefore, it continued. As President Bill Clinton said when asked why he had his affairs, "I did it because I could."

As I pointed out, Pope Francis called priests who abuse children "monsters."

Nelson Mandela said, "Our children are our greatest treasure. They are our future. Those who abuse them tear at the fabric of our society and weaken our nation."

The Roman Catholic Church had a systematic approach to cover up the problem of abusive behavior of its clerical personnel. The documentary *Keepers* is a sad example of the cover-up by the Baltimore diocese and the local police when two priests abused a number of girls for years at a Catholic girls' high school, resulting in the murder and cover-up of a nun who was about to expose them.

Many dioceses are now declaring bankruptcy to be able to pay victims and not take all their funds through law cases.

Should Married People Be Ordained as Priests?

Yes! St. Peter, the first pope, was married, and so were most of the apostles and the followers in the early Church. Remember, celibacy was not mandatory until the eleventh century. The Roman Catholic Church would be much healthier if we allowed married priests. There are many men who would have become priests, but they wanted to get married and have children. We all lose because of obligatory celibacy. Celibacy should be optional. Again, it is more natural to be married. The Roman Catholic Church is very high on what is natural.

Should Women Be Ordained as Priests?

Yes! The argument is that Jesus started the church with the ordination of only men. Would Jesus be an equal-opportunity employer if he were here today? I think so. Women presided at Eucharistic meals in the early church. There is no good reason to not ordain women. The male leadership in the Roman Catholic Church is dragging their feet and are afraid of women being ordained. It is interesting that a good nun friend of mine said she did not want to be ordained a priest because she would then have to be obligated to be under a bishop's control.

Is the Pope Infallible?

No. It was a major mistake to have the pope declared infallible in matters of faith and morals. Back in the First Vatican Council

(1869–70), Pope Pius IX instituted infallibility on July 18, 1870, declaring the Assumption of Mary into heaven. Infallibility is not accepted by other religions and is avoided by many Catholic scholars today.

Should Mary Be Seen as a Virgin and Special in Heaven?

There is no need to see Mary as a virgin after Jesus was born. Why not have Joseph and Mary as a model married couple? If one believes she is the true mother of Jesus and Jesus is the Son of God, it is fitting that she be in a special place in the Catholic religion. People identify with her, and she is seen as human and a source of comfort and an example of a person we should respect in a unique way. Yes, she should be seen as special in heaven. Should a person pray for her intercession? If it makes one feel better, yes. Will she answer? Some people claim that she has appeared to them. In their own minds, they feel she has. I, Thomas the doubter, do not believe she actually has.

It appears that Jesus had brothers and sisters (Matthew 12:46, Luke 8:19, Mark 3:31, Acts 1:14). We were told in school, especially in the seminary, that the brothers were actually cousins. But the word in the Bible used for "brother" in Greek was *adelphos* and not the Greek word for "cousin" *ksadelfos*. That means Mary was the mother of not just Jesus but his brothers and sisters too. I don't feel sorry for Joseph anymore because it looks like he was a normal husband and the father of a number of children.

Is the Roman Catholic Church in Hospice?

Yes! People are leaving the Church throughout the world. Hopefully, Pope Francis will lead people back to the fold.

In the days of my youth, the local parish was the center of our world. People knew one another. We went to school at the Catholic school, played sports, went to Boy and Girl Scouts meetings there, sang in the choir, and did a number of other activities based around the church. We were baptized, went to Sunday Mass, confession and communion, were confirmed, married, and buried from our church. Today many people don't go to church anymore, and if they do, they don't know most of the people there. Those who go to church go through the motions, don't get much out of the sermons, and many don't go to confession anymore. And their children, after leaving the house, don't go to church anymore either. Like the celibate Shakers, the Roman Catholic Church is running out of people and fading fast. The conservatives are taking over, and the overall numbers are decreasing.

Back in 1963, Martin Luther King Jr. asked the question from the Birmingham Jail, "Is organized religion too inextricably bound to the status quo to save our nation and the world?" That is the same question we can ask ourselves today.

An abbot from one of the Benedictine monasteries in the United States made the comment that the Roman Catholic Church, as it presently stands, is in hospice. I, Thomas the doubter, agree.

How About Vocations to the Religious Life?

There is a shortage of priests, brothers, and nuns. This problem is worldwide. As an example, I recently asked the directors of the mother house of two religious orders about new novices. They both said they have not had a woman apply for the past twenty years. One of the Benedictine abbeys in our area has monks who are in their seventies and eighties and very few new young members. There is a different approach to joining the religious life today compared to fifty years ago.

Many of the new priests are very conservative, and some people, as I have said, call them "John Pauls," after the former pope who was very conservative and came from Poland, where the conservative church still has many priests and nuns. Many of the pastors do not want a new assistant because they cause a division in the parish. The older pastor is moderate or liberal, and the new priests are more conservative. The rest of Europe's churches are populated with mostly women and a few old men. People today are more independent and question the traditions of old.

People want us to pray for more vocations to the religious life. Until the Roman Catholic Church agrees to ordain women and allow priests to choose to marry or remain celibate, I do not think things will change for the better.

Does this mean that the people who choose to be a nun, brother, or priest wasted their lives? No. They freely chose to dedicate their lives to prayer and helping others, so it is their own choice, and I am sure they feel their lives are worthwhile and what they wanted to do.

Birth Control

People should be responsible parents. Therefore, they should plan their children to the best of their ability. That means they should practice birth control, and they do. The Roman Catholic Church wants people to use the rhythm method of birth control. It has been proven to be not very reliable. I have had a number of people tell me that their last baby was born using the rhythm method. It almost appears that the Church does not want people to enjoy sex to the point that they are not worried about getting pregnant. Today the Church does come out and say that married people can have sex without always having to expect a possible baby to be the end result.

Contraception can prevent disease, unwanted pregnancies, and allow married people to make love without guilt. The Catholic Church is worried that too many people will enjoy sex and avoid the responsibilities of parenting. It is time for the male clergy to trust adults to make their own personal decisions.

Abortion

I am against abortion. On the other hand, I believe a woman should have a choice about her own body. People again should be educated so that they do not become pregnant. That is easier said than done. If one decides to have an abortion, it should be in the first three months of the pregnancy. Is that a human being? I don't think so. What if there is a miscarriage? Is that a human being? I don't think so. God will take care of any aborted fetus that is a human being. It should be a last resort in a problem situation.

The old joke is, when does life begin? The priest says at conception. The Protestant minister says when the fetus is viable. The rabbi says when the kids move out and the dog dies.

Abortion is a serious matter, and people should take their time and look at all options. Abortion should be the last resort.

Gay Marriage

When two people love each other, there is no reason they cannot get married.

There have been gay people down through the ages. They should be accepted as any other person. God made all of us, gay and straight.

Reincarnation

Despite Shirley MacLaine, I doubt there is reincarnation after death. The joke is that members of the Mafia, organized crime, have to come back to pay for their sins by becoming nuns. Some people say they knew some nuns as they grew up in grade school who could have passed as former Mafia hit men. I wonder if people who die young and never had a chance to live come back for a fairer opportunity to enjoy life. It seems only right.

Prayer

Does it do any good to pray? It does make the person who prays feel better and the person they pray for if they are told that someone is praying for them. Psychologically, they also feel better. Does God or the saints hear our prayers? Will God, Mary or one of the other saints, as I have said before, find you that parking spot or help you pass a test or get that job? I believe God has given us life and it is up to us to use our God given talents. God is not going to perform our own special miracle.

Did God call me to be a priest? I chose to become a priest because I was following the model that my pastor and the nuns were portraying to best serve God's people. That's why when I saw the tradition of obligatory celibacy made no sense for me, I chose to resign, marry, have a family and become a criminal justice specialist and help victims of crime and try to have offenders be accountable for their choices. I chose to become a priest. I was not knocked off my horse like Saint Paul. I also chose to resign and become a lay person.

The Case Against Organized Religion

Organized religion has the problem of any group of people who exist for a period of time and become too set in their ways. This is true in government, unions, higher education, social clubs, and a number of other areas in our world. The top people become too powerful and are not ready to change. That is an argument for term limits in government. I am for unions, but leadership there can be too powerful and one-sided and forget to serve the members and instead fight for individuals who are not doing the job. Try to fire a union member for legitimate reasons. University professors with tenure sit back and do research and can forget to be in the classroom where the students need him or her. Publish or perish.

The same is true in religion. Some people need to go to a regular service for their own comfort, but religions too get stuck in their traditional ways. Roman Catholic priests, bishops, archbishops, cardinals, and even the popes practice clericalism, tradition, and forget about the people they have chosen to serve.

People have told me that if you are disillusioned with the Roman Catholic Church, try another religion. Same problem. I prefer to create my community with my family, friends, coworkers, neighbors, reading, hiking, and enjoying nature and the beauty of creation instead of sitting in a large building hearing holy words put together with people I do not know.

In America, 3,500 to 4,000 churches close their doors each year. One thousand and four hundred pastors in America leave the ministry monthly according to "Death by Ministry" by Darin Patrick.

At a funeral, I prefer to stand with the bereaved rather than pray for the deceased. At a wedding, I choose to celebrate with the couple, whether it is in a religious ceremony or before a judge. It is up to the couple how their married life will turn out.

In a *Time* magazine article (June 19, 2017), Elizabeth Diaz writes about the God squad. It is a number of young priests who are trying to energize the Catholic Church. However, at the same time, there are people who are trying to keep the Catholic Church very conservative and limited to like-minded people. Even the Vatican and Pope Francis are warning about this type of thinking.

Each person has to decide for herself or himself whether they need organized religion or not. If a person is comforted by going to a church, synagogue, mosque, or commune with nature, more power to them.

G.K. Chesterton stated "The Christian ideal has been tried and found wanting. It has been found difficult and left untried."

Mortal and Venial Sins

Here is another method to control human behavior. Is it a serious matter not to go to church every Sunday? It is a good way to get people to come to church and put their offering in the collection basket. With a mortal sin, we were told that if we died with that type of stain on our soul that we had not confessed to a priest, we would go to hell. I don't think anybody in heaven is keeping book on us down here on earth. That idea was certainly an incentive to keep us on the right side of the rules and get to the sacrament of penance as soon as you could.

The joke was told that two people in hell were talking to each other. One said, "I am in hell because I was a hit man and killed a number of people. I robbed banks, sold drugs, and ran houses of prostitution." When the other person was asked what he had done to get sent to hell, he said he ate meat on Friday.

A venial sin is less serious but a good thing to confess so you would not be doing it all the time. To tell a little white lie is not a good habit to get into.

I remember my first experience with hearing the confessions of children as I stated before. It was an eye-awaking experience how the sacrament of penance should not be experienced.

After six years as a priest, we were holding communal penance, and after a brief examination of an individual's responsibilities, we would have them come up for personal absolution in English. Those who wanted to talk to a priest could stay and go into the confessional or a room set aside to go through the screen or just go around the kneeler and sit face-to-face with the priest. It didn't take long, and we were called into the archbishop's office and told we could not do that anymore. I can remember a number of people coming up after we had started the open sacrament of penance with tears in their eyes and smiles on their faces. I am told by priests serving today that not too many people go to confession anymore.

Relics

I doubt that relics have any value or power. Pieces of bone, a head of a saint, or even a preserved body are just that. And in many cases, the so-called relic is not what it is claimed to be. For example, the Shroud of Turin, believed by some to show the face of Christ at his crucifixion, has been investigated and tested with mixed results. When people could not read or write, relics served as a sign of contact with the saint and was real for the common man or woman. They could see the relic, and it helped them identify with that saint and hope that through this contact, their prayers could be answered. When we traveled to Croatia in 2016, our guide took us into a private side room in the front of the local church, and we saw hundreds of relics encased in what looked like gold but must have been brass. They went from the floor to the ceiling. In the Middle Ages, there were princes who collected as many relics as they could to outdo the neighboring prince. Today there are relics in most Catholic churches, but it appears that there is limited interest in their value.

Transubstantiation

My father said he worked so hard on the farm that he worked a hump on his back, and then he worked so hard he worked the hump off (he was a farmer and a full-time police officer). He also said, "Your mother works her fingers to the bone, cleaning, washing, and preparing food for a family of five growing boys. So clean your plate and be grateful." We always cleaned our plates. When I heard of transubstantiation, I thought of my father's words. When we attend Mass, Jesus said he is with us. The bread is not necessarily his body and the wine his blood, but Jesus is with us as we give thanks (the Eucharist), just as my father and mother were there pouring themselves into our family meal. In turn, Jesus is with us at Mass as we break the bread of life and drink the cup of salvation. That is as close to transubstantiation as I can come. Some who are nonbelievers say that we must be part-cannibal to eat the body of Christ and vampires to drink his blood.

Is It God's Will?

One often hears that bad or good things happen, and the answer is that it is God's will. God gives us life and lets us live it. What we do with it is our own doing. I doubt that all the tragedies that happen all over the world are God's will. God could interfere but does not.

Conclusion

Once again, I am not losing my faith. Doubt is part of faith. I will also say it again: indifference is the opposite of faith. I am not indifferent. I am very concerned about life and the meaning of life.

Everyone has to live their own life. God gives us the freedom to do this. When I pass away from this life, I plan to have my body given to science. I hope my soul or spirit goes to the happy hunting grounds. If organized religion helps you to live your life better, then more power to you. If you believe in God as your Creator and there is an afterlife, perhaps we will meet again, and you can say, "I told you so." If this is all we get, then live your life to the fullest and remember we are all sisters and brothers in the human family. Love your neighbor as yourself.

Acknowledgements

I would like to thank the following people for the help and ideas on this book. It does not mean that they all agreed with me as I put my thoughts and experiences together.

Firstly, I would like to thank my wife, Bernice. Next, I would like to recognize my sons Craig, Andrew, and my daughter, Jen, and their spouses Jessica, Paula, and Brandon, and my grandchildren Anderson, Beckett, Abigail, Elliott, and Audrey. They have been my inspiration and support.

I would also like to thank all my classmates, friends, teachers, and priests, brothers, nuns—both present-day and those who have resigned over the years.

In addition, I am grateful to religious leaders, ministers, nuns, brothers and rabbis of other religions, and laypeople whom I have met and known and learned from in discussions about our beliefs.

I would like to thank friends Diane Corey for her help with the computer work and Pat Mulvehill, Bob Schmainda and Father Ray Monsour for their frank and open discussions.

I would like to thank the legal help I have received from my brother Ed (Loophole) Christian, and my son Craig and daughter in law Jessica Cohen.

About the Author

Thomas Frank Christian served as a Roman Catholic priest for six years and then resigned because he did not agree with obligatory celibacy. He became a probation counselor, ran alternatives to incarceration programs, and retired after working thirty-five years as a criminal justice specialist in four states. In 1979, he was voted the Minnesota Corrections Professional of the Year. For fifteen years, he was the state director of the Community Dispute Resolution Centers Program for the New York State Unified Court System, administrating criminal, civil, and family cases.

His publications include a series of articles and three books in his field. Degrees include a master's degree and PhD from Michigan State University School of Criminal Justice.

Instructional career includes teaching at the University of Minnesota and Mankato State University, and he has lectured at many colleges and universities.

He has mediated victim-and-offender cases on *48 Hours*, Home Box Office, and National Public Radio.

He and his wife have three children and five grandchildren.

CPSIA information can be obtained
at www.ICGtesting.com
Printed in the USA
BVHW02*1945041018
527996BV00019B/18/P